WRITERS AND THEIR WORK

ISOBEL ARMSTRONG
General Editor

JANE AUSTEN

Mrs William Urquhart

A portrait (1814 - 1815) of Mrs William Urquhart in oil on canvas by
Sir Henry Raeburn (1756 - 1823) by courtesy of Glasgow Museums:
Art Gallery & Museum, Kelvingrove.

Author's note. *The cover picture by Cassandra is the only authenticated portrait we
have of Jane Austen. By all accounts Cassandra's portrait is not a reliable image and
the family were not fond of it. To balance Cassandra's delusive likeness I offer, as a
frontispiece, not another invented image, but a picture by Henry Raeburn, one of the
leading portrait painters of Jane Austen's day. "Mrs Urquhart" dates from the period
in which* EMMA *was written and may be considered a visual equivalent of Austen's
unrivalled art of producing personality.*

W

JANE AUSTEN

Robert Miles

Northcote House
in association with the
British Council

© Copyright 2003 by Robert Miles

First published in 2003 by Northcote House Publishers Ltd, Horndon, Tavistock, Devon, PL19 9NQ, United Kingdom. Tel: +44 (01822) 810066. Fax: +44 (01822) 810034.

British Library Cataloguing-in-Publication Data
A catalogue record for this book is available from the British Library

ISBN 0-7463-0767-5 hardcover
ISBN 0-7463-0876-0 paperback

Typeset by TW Typesetting, Plymouth, Devon
Printed and bound in the United Kingdom

Contents

Acknowledgements

Jane Austen was written with the generous assistance of the Arts and Humanities Research Board.

I would like to thank Alison Chapman for her advice on the frontispiece; Faye Hammill, who made a timely intervention; Anthony Mandal and Joseph Bray, who both generously shared their own work-in-progress with me; but above all Richard Cronin, whose conversation in the Rubaiyat was an instructional delight, and who read the manuscript with an expert eye.

Biographical Outline

1775   Born, 16 December, at Steventon, Hampshire, the daughter of the Revd George Austen (1731–1805) and Cassandra Leigh (1739–1827). Jane is the seventh of eight children, two girls and six boys: James (1765–1819), George (1766–1838), Edward (1768–1852), Henry (1771–1850), Cassandra (1773–1845), Francis (1774–1865) and Charles (1779–1852).

1781   Eliza, the daughter of George Austen's half-sister, Philadelphia Hancock (*née* Walter), marries Jean Capote, Comte de Feuillide.

1783   Jane and Cassandra sent with their cousin Jane Cooper to study with Mrs. Cawley, in Southampton, where Jane catches a 'putrid fever' (probably diptheria).

1784   Jane and Cassandra return home to Steventon.

1785–7   Jane and Cassandra attend the Abbey School, Reading.

1788   Warren Hastings impeached for corruption by the House of Lords for his administration of British India: the trial lasts seven years. Hastings was a close friend of George Austen's half-sister, Philadelphia Hancock. George Austen acted as foster father for Hastings's son, for three years, before the boy's death of diphtheria, aged 6. On Hancock's death Hastings settled a £10,000 trust on Philadelphia, suggesting that the boy was their offspring. There is also a question mark about whether Philadelphia's daughter, Eliza Hancock, was also Hastings's child.

1789–91	Writes juvenilia: 'Love and Freindship', a 'History of England', and the stories 'Lesley Castle' and 'A Collection of Letters'.
1792	Writes 'Catharine'.
1793	Edward Austen (Jane's third eldest brother) inherits the properties of Godmersham, in Kent, and Chawton, in Hampshire, from Thomas Knight, a kinsman of George Austen.
1794	Begins 'Lady Susan'. Warren Hastings acquitted after a seven-year trial. The Count de Feuillide, husband of Jane's cousin, Eliza, guillotined in Paris: Eliza moves to Steventon with her invalid child.
1795	Begins 'Elinor and Marianne' (an early version of *Sense and Sensibility*).
1796	January: meets Tom Lefroy, her first romantic interest. Frances Burney publishes *Camilla*.
1797	Finishes *First Impressions* (an early version of *Pride and Prejudice*) and offers it to the London publisher Thomas Cadell, who turns it down; instead Cadell publishes Ann Radcliffe's *The Italian*, paying £800 for the copyright, an unprecedented sum. Cassandra's fiancé, Thomas Fowle, dies of yellow fever in the West Indies. At the invitation of Thomas Knight's widow, Edward Austen takes possession of the estates at Godmersham and Chawton. Henry Austen marries his cousin, the Comtesse de Feuillide (*née* Eliza Hancock).
1797–8	Rewrites 'Elinor and Marianne' as *Sense and Sensibility*. In November visits Bath with her mother.
1798–9	Writes *Susan*, the first version of *Northanger Abbey*.
1799	Visits Bath during May and June with her mother and her brother Edward and his family. Jane Austen's aunt, Jane Leigh-Perrot, accused of stealing lace from a Bath shop, a felony punishable by death or transportation. Mrs Leigh-Perrot spends eight months in gaol before being acquitted by a jury after a fifteen-minute deliberation.
1800	Writes a brief, dramatized version of Samuel Richardson's *Sir Charles Grandison*, her favourite novel.

1801	The Austens move from Steventon to Bath.
1802	2 December, receives and rejects a proposal of marriage from Harris Bigg Wither of Manydown.
1803	The copyright of *Susan* sold to the publisher Crosby for £10, but Crosby declines to publish the novel.
1804–5	Writes 'The Watsons'. Frank Austen made commander of the *Leopard* and then of the *Canopus*.
1804	Revd George Austen dies, 21 January.
1805	Jane, Cassandra, and Mrs Austen move to Southampton where they live with Frank Austen and his wife. Frank Austen made commander of the *St Albans*.
1808	Receives and rejects a proposal of marriage from Edward Bridges, a clergyman, and brother of Elizabeth Austen, Edward Austen's wife. Elizabeth Austen dies after delivering her eleventh child.
1809	Jane, Cassandra, and Mrs Austen move to Chawton cottage on the Hampshire estate of Edward Austen.
1811	*Sense and Sensibility* published by Thomas Egerton.
1813	*Pride and Prejudice* published by Thomas Egerton.
1814	*Mansfield Park* published by Thomas Egerton.
1816	*Emma* published by John Murray. In March Sir Walter Scott's laudatory review of *Emma* appears in the *Quarterly Review*. The copyright of *Susan* purchased back from Crosby. On 23 March 1816 Henry Austen made bankrupt after the failure of the Alton Bank: Edward Knight loses £20,000, Jane, £13. Completes *Persuasion* on 16 July. Jane Austen ill with Addison's disease, a form of tuberculosis that effects the adrenal glands.
1817	Jane Austen dies of her illness, 18 July, aged 41, in Winchester. Her last work, 'Sanditon', is left as a fragment.
1818	*Northanger Abbey* and *Persuasion* published by John Murray.

Abbreviations and References

E.   *Emma*, ed. Fiona Stafford (Harmondsworth: Penguin, 1996)

MP   *Mansfield Park*, ed. Kathyrn Sutherland (Harmondsworth: Penguin, 1996)

NA   *Northanger Abbey*, ed. Marilyn Butler (Harmondsworth: Penguin, 1995)

P.   *Persuasion*, ed. Gillian Beer (Harmondsworth: Penguin, 1998)

PP   *Pride and Prejudice*, ed. Vivien Jones (Harmondsworth: Penguin, 1996)

SS   *Sense and Sensibility*, ed. Ros Ballaster (Harmondsworth: Penguin, 1995)

Introduction

> If one thinks of it, it is *only* Jane Austen (no longer Charles
> Lamb to the same extent or even Dickens, and we don't
> love Dr. Johnson though his life is incessantly being
> investigated) – only Jane Austen who is loved and
> esteemed by her readers as a *person*. Isn't it because,
> through her writings alone, we acquire the impression of
> a delightful personality and admirable character, in spite
> of the impersonality of the novels?
>
> Q. D. Leavis[1]

It is one of the great clichés of Austen criticism that no other
English writer is quite so English as Jane Austen. The point of
this cliché is not that Austen really is more 'English' than other
writers: it is that she is generally perceived to be so. The critic
Roger Gard puts it thus: 'most of her readers, whatever their
nationality, are likely to be mildly pleased by being told, quite
often, that she is very English.'[2] Austen's Englishness delights
non-native readers because they have a great appetite for the
England of rose-covered cottages, eighteenth-century villages,
parsonages, large aristocratic homes, eccentric members of the
royal family, and Beefeaters in red coats and preposterous
hats, into which Austen somehow nicely fits. English readers
who find it agreeable to consider Jane Austen the embodiment
of the verities of English country life are swelled by the
national pride that comes with possessing such a treasure, a
novelist whose cleverness and wit can never really be appreci-
ated, not properly, by the non-native reader. For the English
reader, Austen is very much 'our thing'. The greater the
refinement of the irony, the greater the reader's identification

1

with what is precious and intangible in the mysterium that has made – that has always made – England, England. For the 'mildly pleased' English reader, referred to by Gard, there is a recognition, although never put in such direct terms, that Austen's irony really is *sui generis*. If it takes 500 years of assiduous rolling to produce a proper bit of lawn, it certainly takes an equally long time to produce a writer capable of spinning bons mots of the same calibre as Austen's.

This proud species of Austen reader is often referred to (and not always with strict accuracy) as a 'Janeite',[3] while the less discriminating fan of Austenian Englishness is said to be a consumer of the heritage industry, meaning places where one can visit authentic Georgian villages with wax mannequins placed *in situ*, with a walkman piping authoritatively in one's ear, or watch something similar on BBC 2, with all the actors dressed in real period costumes, as validated by the Victoria and Albert Museum.[4]

Almost without exception, the vast library of critical works that has grown up around Austen, in recent years, begins with a gallant effort to rescue the writer from the heritage industry or from the Janeites. A proud tradition of critical interventions has endeavoured to render Austen strange or somehow not 'English'. Margaret Oliphant and Richard Simpson sought to bring the prickly novelist out from beneath the cosy guise of the maiden aunt and Vicar's tea companion that had been thrust upon her by her nephew's hagiographical memoir of 1870,[5] but the first really significant attempt was made by the psychologist, critic, and member of F. R. Leavis's *Scrutiny* group, D. W. Harding.[6] In 'Regulated Hatred', a now famous essay, Harding argued that Austen did not idealize her society (the three or four country families in which she moved, and about whom she recommended writing) so much as she dissected them with a forensic wit. Indicting her neighbours of moral sloth and ethical degeneracy was, Harding argued, an essential psychological strategy of the novelist. By exercising her hatred through controlled expenditures of poison Austen was able to regulate her emotions, a form of writing cure where the alternative was to suffer the surfeit of bile her provincial surroundings doubtless produced. As an example of what Harding means, consider the following description of Lady Middleton from *Sense and Sensibility*:

Though nothing could be more polite than Lady Middleton's behaviour to Elinor and Marianne, she did not really like them at all. Because they neither flattered herself nor her children, she could not believe them good-natured; and because they were fond of reading, she fancied them satirical: perhaps without exactly knowing what it was to be satirical; but *that* did not signify. It was a censure in common use, and easily given. (*SS* 207)

The narrator's jab is 'satirical' in a way Lady Middleton is incapable of understanding. Its primary target is the disjunction between letter and spirit – between form and whatever it is that gives form meaning and value – in Lady Middleton's manners and understanding. Thus in the first sentence affection and politeness are separate things, while in the next social commerce has become a one-way interaction where Lady Middleton's positive regard is simply flattery on the rebound. It would not be true to say that Lady Middleton is completely without an inner life, as the narrator takes us inside her head, mimicking her speech rhythms with 'but *that* did not signify. It was a censure in common use, and easily given.' The phrasing displays the effortless cadence of cliché, of phrasing that comes easily, regardless of sense. The final satiric twist of 'easily given' is particularly deadly. In a general way it echoes Lady Middleton's selfishness, her strenuous avoidance of that which is not easily given, of that which costs. In this specific instance 'easily given' refers back to 'censure'. In so far as censure involves bad feelings it is always 'easily given'. Self-evidently, Lady Middleton's censure is no more a moral act than a lustful impulse would be (also something 'easily given'). Read as Lady Middleton's, the phrase is a piece of meaningless cant; read as the narrator's, it is a sharp reminder of Lady Middleton's moral nullity.

Harding argued that Austen was full of these quiet acts of ironic assassination. I have picked this particular example as it helps to illustrate Harding's other point, one highly vexatious to the *Scrutiny* circle of critics of which Harding was a part, which is that the Janeites who laid claim to the strongest ownership of the writer appeared to be the very readers who were the least able, and even, arguably, the least fit, to read her. It was as if the Lady Middletons of this world had clubbed together to promote their dear, sweet, 'satirical' Jane as the

3

desirable epitome of their English, Home Counties way of life, inanely boasting of what they did not understand, and would not like, if they did. Harding's mission was to rescue Austen from these complacent literary vandals. Since Harding, a number of critics have taken up the task of establishing Austen's uncomfortable prickliness: Marvin Murdrick's *Jane Austen* and John Halperin's *The Life of Jane Austen* are both good examples.[7]

If one strand of Austen criticism sets out to prove that the writer is not so nice or so cosily English as she seems, or others take her for, another has tried to make her appear strange, breaking open the crust of familiarity that has gathered around her. This has been an even more resourceful branch of Austen criticism. In his last essay on Austen, the American critic Lionel Trilling adopted the gambit of approaching the Georgian writer anthropologically, invoking Clifford Geertz's ethnographic 'thick description' on the premise that Austen's culture was now so remote from ours, it might as well be Melanesian as English.[8] More recently Edward Said has set the fox among the heritage chickens by arguing that Austen colluded with the system of slavery underwriting British Imperial wealth, much as it does the Bertram fortune in *Mansfield Park*. In Said's reading, Fanny's move from the periphery to the centre of the Bertram family is a doubling of Sir Thomas's renovating return from the family's (and therefore the country's) sugar-producing hinterland: but by foregrounding this movement in familial terms the novel normalized and obscured the material realities involved in empire.[9] As such, Said's argument is really just another instance of the strand of criticism that argues that Austen's works are fully imbricated within history and politics as a means of counteracting the view that Austen's works do not trespass the limits of the drawing room.

More sensationally still, Terry Castle, a professor of English from Stanford, argued in the *London Review of Books* that Austen's relationship with her sister Cassandra was, at the very least, homosocial, an argument that somehow became an accusation in the media ballyhoo that followed this attack on the national treasure, with Professor Castle arraigned on national TV through a live satellite link, with the distinguished British expert, Professor Marilyn Butler, brought into the studio to act, with evident reluctance, as the voice of reason.[10] Castle has not been alone in her desire to invert the traditional image of Austen as the 'bovine, well-disposed, sweet-tempered, humanity-loving woman depicted by the family'.[11] For D. W. Miller, Austen's polished, epigrammatic style has been misunderstood. Miller argues that critics have interpreted the creativity of her style – its impenetrable aesthetic surface – as a compensation for, and hence a defence against, her spinsterhood. For Miller, such a view uncritically reflects the heterosexual norm. He sees Austen's art, rather, as a 'will to style' linked to 'the felt unrepresentability of her situation'. Miller reads Austen as aggressively asserting her anomalous identity through the aesthetic surfaces of her writing, and in so doing he links her to Oscar Wilde and to a tradition of radical, gay, aesthetics.[12]

Even within this dissident tradition of Austen criticism there has been something of the 'our-Jane' syndrome; at least, so it may seem if one concentrates on reaction to Marilyn Butler's highly influential *Jane Austen and the War of Ideas*.[13] Butler was in the vanguard of the critical effort to disprove the complacent assumption that Austen was innocent of politics and, as her title suggests, ideas. Rather than a retired spinster vicariously living her proper destiny through her obsessive marriage plots, Butler's Austen is a feisty intellectual combatant in the febrile, highly politicized atmosphere of post-French-Revolutionary Britain. Butler's critics have been delighted with this image of Austen the political writer. They have been less comfortable with the kind of politics Butler has her staunchly defending: the rational, Anglican ones of country Tories. For many critics Butler's Austen was worryingly close to the traditional image of Austen the small 'c' conservative English countrywoman. Those who have taken issue with Butler have thus tried to show how Austen might be convicted of the taint of subversion, through complicity with the radical edges of the Romantic sensibility, or by establishing through careful scholarship Austen's affinity with the emergent feminism to be found in a growing community of sister novelists.[14] Austen, it seems, inspires powerful identifications; and it is the nature of such identification to find in its object something of what the individual brings to it.

5

An easy response to the phenomenon of contradictory interpretations is to say that, after all, Austen was an imaginative novelist and it is the nature of novelists to argue both sides of the toss, that what we have is less a matter of outright contradiction, more one of contrary emphases. But that is not what I wish to argue. I think it indubitably true that Austen's ideological centre of gravity was Anglican and small 't' tory. I believe it is informative to know this; but that is not what I shall address in this book. There has been a great deal of excellent criticism in recent years, which has sought to fix Austen in her time and place. And it has done so, not by taking Austen out of the parlour, but by turning the parlour into something else: into the work space of the professional women writer.[15] The 'new' Jane Austen is a woman serious about the business of writing and as such directly connected to her fellow professionals and to the world of commerce in its widest sense. Austen may have been an Anglican and Tory by birth, culture, and affirmation, but she was a writer by profession, and a woman writer at that. All three things provide scope for ideological contradiction, so we should not be surprised that Austen's works are slippery things when it comes to pinning down their affiliations.[16]

In various ways, then, Austen criticism has sought to release Austen from the sterile environs of the heritage industry, freeing her into something like the fully nuanced complexity of her cultural moment, where her writing is allowed to run satirically free. While I am sympathetic to, and informed by, this body of criticism, it is not my aim to contribute to it, at least, not directly. Rather, in this book I will be concerned with a different question: what is it about Jane Austen's work that has provoked such strong identifications? Referring back to the epigraph by Q. D. Leavis, why is 'Jane', the person, the most loved of English writers? And what about her writings identifies her as 'English'?

There are several aspects to my answer to these questions, each one a subject of the chapters that follow. But before I take these aspects in turn, it may be helpful if I broadly sketch my argument. My starting point is also to be found in the quotation from Q. D. Leavis. By the 'impersonality of the novels' Leavis means Austen's famous irony, the satiric aloofness with which she plays out rope to her characters. Despite this impersonality, says Leavis, a delightful sense of the author's character comes through the writing. I want to put the matter differently and say that the source of these strong Austenian identifications lies with the novelist's ability to create the illusion of personality. As any reader of Austen will know, an Austen novel is filled with three different kinds of characters: personalities, grotesques, and those who hover in between. The personalities and grotesques are easy to name. The former encompasses Elinor Dashwood, Elizabeth Bennet, Fanny Price, Emma Woodhouse, and Anne Elliott: in other words, the heroines (apart from Catherine Morland, whom I think a special case). The grotesques are legion: but, as a sample, we might consider Mr Collins, Isabella Thorpe, Mrs Norris, Sir Walter Elliot, Mr and Mrs John Dashwood, and Mrs Elton. The romantic heroes (and even the romantic villains) never cross over into the grotesque category. But neither are they self-evidently 'personalities'. Why this is so is technically complex, as it has to do with shifts in point of view. At this stage suffice to say that the more the romantic hero wins the heroine's approval, the more he takes on the aspect of a personality. An Austen novel is a dynamic space in which personalities, and grotesques, collide. Within this space we are invited to bond with the heroine, the lead personality. So strong is this invitation, and so charmed, and complex, the personality, it is difficult to resist concluding that in her heroines one encounters something of Austen herself. Patricia Rozema's film version of *Mansfield Park* (1999) offers a case in point, as Fanny Price finds her character subtly (and not so subtly) adapted in order to appear as the director's version of Fanny's author (thus imparting glamour to Austen's most problematically uncharismatic heroine). And for what I shall argue are themselves very involved reasons, this charmed Austenian personality, that passes successively from heroine to heroine, is herself a tantalizing embodiment of Englishness.

But for the moment I wish to stay with the concept of personality. We are so used to thinking of novels in terms of character that we often take the achievement of personality in fiction as a matter of course, indeed, so much so that 'character analysis' is generally regarded as a pre-critical response to fiction, something undergraduates automatically bring with them, of which, equally automatically, they have to be broken. However, if we consider the achievement of personality historically, it becomes a far more interesting topic. In fiction, characters are not born, but made; and they have not always been made the same way. Moreover, the ability to create characters who appear to come alive, leaving the stage or page to inhabit the minds of their auditors and readers, to carry on there an independent existence, is itself a historically specific skill. Thus Harold Bloom's recent argument in *Shakespeare: The Invention of the Human* (1999). As Bloom sees it, Shakespeare's genius was to be the first to create a dramaturgical, fictional language for the expression of the human; indeed it is through Shakespeare, and Shakespeare's legacy, that we come to know the human at all. For Bloom, we are all Shakespeareans now, for it is Shakespeare who has made our humanity manifest. Shakespeare's host of complex and dynamic characters, his 'personalities', provide the templates through which we know ourselves, our desires, our noble aspirations, as well as our foibles, deceits, evasions, and repressions.[17]

Bloom's book has met with a very mixed reception. There have been some rave reviews, some hostile ones, and a degree of silence. However, it has been something of a popular success; at any rate, it had the uncommon distinction for a book of criticism of having been displayed prominently, and in bulk, in the kinds of bookshops that usually devote this kind of attention to best-sellers. Bloom's book has drawn hostility from the more theory-minded critics, who have seen *The Invention of the Human* as a regressive return to character analysis, to an obfuscating form of hagiography, in which illusory notions of Western subjectivity come to the fore, rather than a proper analysis of texts and cultural provenance. Bloom, in return, has characterized his critics as 'resentniks' haunting the 'swamps' of 'cultural studies'.

Without endorsing the attacks on Bloom's book, I want to distance myself from it. I do see Austen following on from Shakespeare as a brilliant creator of fictional character, but this has been a common observation in Austen criticism since the nineteenth century. For instance, in 1870 Goldwin Smith observed the following of Shakespeare and Austen:

Both are really creative, both purely artistic; both have the marvellous power of endowing the products of their imagination with a life, as it were, apart from their own. Each holds up a perfectly clear and undistorting mirror – Shakespeare to the moral universe, Austen to the little world in which she lived. In the case of neither does the personality of the author ever come between the spectator and the drama.[19]

While supporting the drift of Smith's remarks, I emphatically do not see this as a matter of discovering the human, in the sense of disclosing a universal nature already there (in this respect Smith's mirror metaphor must be approached with caution). I think it is possible to speak of a universal human nature. But our universal nature is banal, fictionally speaking, precisely because it is universal. Fictions are inescapably cultural artefacts, which is what makes them interesting. Austen's way of imagining the human is particular, not just to her place in history – meaning her location on a small imperial island at a crucial juncture in the rise of Western hegemony – but to her place in literary history. Her personalities are not made out of the raw stuff of the human condition; they are fabricated out of a raft of fictional techniques, which she inherited, and which she, in various important ways, pushed further.

I can perhaps throw into relief the substance of the previous paragraph by referring to an anecdote related by Lionel Trilling in his last essay on Austen. The point of Trilling's anecdote was to illustrate cultural difference. It concerned the mores of the ancient Thai people. As Buddhists, a great value was placed on harmonizing inside and outside, one's inner feelings and one's outward behaviour. To master this principle was to behave at all times in a ritualized fashion, with an even tranquillity. As an example of the triumphant achievement of this principle Trilling cites the case of a newly married young man. Although recently bereaved through a tragic mishap, the young man continued to behave with the serene equanimity with which he habitually conducted his life, an example much lauded by his peers. Trilling's point in reciting this story was to emphasize how culturally specific our notions of normal behaviour are. From a Western standpoint, the young man's actions appear incomprehensible, or worse, psychotic. But one could also relate the anecdote to culturally specific notions of personality. Adopting a Western perspective, one might conclude that the young man did not have one. It runs with the grain of Western thought to believe that it is through the unevenness of our lives that personality is especially known. The matter is more complex, and richer, than might at first appear, for the notion of personality as a test – where moral fibre is known through encounters with that which challenges – has its broad origins in Christianity, and perhaps more narrowly, and latterly, in Protestantism. To grasp the last point, one need think only of Bunyan's *Pilgrim's Progress*. There is also within our culture vestiges of what one might call the Romantic self, the belief, avidly subscribed to by Marianne Dashwood, that our spiritual mettle is tested by our ability to respond joyfully or with great sorrow to life's vicissitudes.

It is not my purpose here to investigate the very involved topic of Western notions of personality. My concern, rather, is with how Jane Austen creates the illusion of personality within her fictions. The 'illusion' is of crucial importance, for, although Austen invites us to consider her characters as 'real people', she does so within the limited context of judging the moral weight of their actions. In other words, the illusion serves the purposes of fiction. Once we lose sight of this, and drift into talking of Austen's characters devoid of their fictional contexts, we begin to go badly wrong. In pursuing the question of how Austen creates the illusion of personality, then, we have to bear a number of things in mind. First, the notion of personality with which Austen works is specific to a place and time. Secondly, it is grounded in the social and material particularities of Austen's culture, by which I mean issues of class, money, and gender. Thirdly, it is profoundly influenced by the medium through which she achieves the illusion of personality: the conventions of the novel.

These three things, then, are the matter of chapters 1–4. In chapter 1 I elaborate further on the concept of personality in fiction; in chapter 2, I relate personality to the specifics of Austen's use of genre. Chapter 3 focuses on Austen's pioneering use of free indirect speech, which is where Austen's technical innovations in the area of the novel come together with her achievement of the illusion of personality. Chapter 4 shows how technical innovation and the illusion of personality combine to constitute Austen's historically specific representations of class, gender, and national self-consciousness. My Conclusion returns to the question raised at the beginning of my Introduction: what is it about Jane Austen's work that has provoked such strong identifications among her readers? Why is 'Jane', the person, the most loved of English writers? And what about her writings identifies her as 'English'?

Criticism may be divided into commentary and critique. By 'commentary' I mean criticism that sets out to understand a work in its own terms. Thus, for instance, a commentary on an epic would consider the work within the generic conventions and expectations it invites. A critique, on the other hand, seeks to place, and interpret, the terms the work invokes. In the case of a would-be epic, such as, say, Whitman's *Song of Myself*, a critique would consider, not whether Whitman's poem was successful as an epic, but why an epic: what about Whitman's moment made the epic form necessary for Whitman's purposes, and what does Whitman's use of the epic form tell us about the culture out of which it arose? Most works of criticism combine a mixture of commentary and critique, and this book is no exception. I should say, however, that the first three chapters are mostly commentary, in that they discuss Austen's work within its own terms. But, as we shall see in chapter 4 and the Conclusion, this is preparatory for a switch to critique, which is what we need to do if we are to answer the questions I have posed in this Introduction.[19]

1

Personality in Austen

The concept of personality has been surprisingly unexplored by literary critics, although more has been written on 'character'.[1] The concept of character may encompass any fictional agent, whether human, animal, or even (in children's stories) vegetable or mineral. Personality, by contrast, is a much more limited category. By personality I mean the creation of the illusion of personhood in fiction, the deceptive feeling we get that we know the people we encounter in a fictional world as well as we know anyone, including, perhaps, ourselves. Shared illusions are culture specific. If an author's textual marionettes come to life for us, it is partly because they gratify collective expectations of what a person should be. As mentioned in the Introduction, I want to put the larger issue to one side in order to focus on the narrower question of why the trick of personality was central to Austen's purposes.

One of Austen's great nineteenth-century critics, Richard Simpson, described Austen's attitude towards character like this:

> Hence again the individual mind can only be represented by her as a battle-field, where contending hosts are marshalled, and where victory inclines now to one side, now to another. A character therefore unfolded itself to her, not in statuesque repose, not as a model without motion, but as a dramatic sketch, a living history, a composite force, which could only exhibit what it was by exhibiting what it did.[2]

Barbara Hardy provides a gloss for Simpson that is as helpful as it is deceptively simple: the illusion of personality in fiction depends on characters changing according to the company they keep.[3] We categorize characters who do not change as caricatures or grotesques: as creations subservient to comic or satiric purposes. In his book on laughter the nineteenth-century French philosopher Henri Bergson famously located one source of the comic in the perception of the mechanical within the human, of simplicity, where we expect complexity. Such laughter tends towards the nervous, or angry, kind.[4] Thus, in *Mansfield Park*, Aunt Norris may change according to the company she addresses – sycophantic to Sir Thomas, mollycoddling to Maria, and viciously patronizing to Fanny – but in this as in everything else she is entirely predictable as she finds herself caught within the mechanical grip of her predominating vices: envy, jealousy, and overweening self-importance. As such she is a grotesque rather than a personality, a 'flat' rather than a 'round' character, to use E. M. Forster's once-popular terms.[5]

Aunt Norris is incapable of moderating her behaviour as the company changes as she lacks a psychology, an inner life, the ability to introspect, to weigh up her own motives, the apparent motives of others, and to act accordingly. In the grip of her prevailing vices, she acts mechanically. To put it another way, she is incapable of scheming, as her vices immediately get the better of the delayed gratification scheming requires. Austen's personalities, on the other hand, do have an inner life. On the whole, this inwardness is indirectly disclosed to us. Early on in the novel Emma Woodhouse behaves differently when she is in Mr Knightley's company, as opposed to Mr Elton's or Harriet Smith's, and we are left to infer what this difference means. In *Sense and Sensibility*, Elinor is so guarded in the presence of Lucy Steele that she seems hardly the same, frank person we had become accustomed to. It is left to the reader to figure out what is happening below the surface of the narration, and, while Austen – or her narrator – may eventually tell us, it is frequently only after we have had the opportunity of surmising it ourselves. A frequent reason why characters do change according to the company they keep is that they are indeed scheming. Even 'good' Fanny Price has her own inner demons – her own jealousies, desires, and fears – which she keeps carefully hidden, and which make her behaviour a puzzle to others.

13

We read Austen's characters, then, as we read other persons, with their own desires, ambitions, and viewpoints, which for various reasons they modify, enhance, deny, or simply lie about, and which we, in the ordinary course of social events, attempt to interpret, as best we can. This dynamic sense of selfhood is the quick of Austen's illusion of personality, as created in her novels. Her characters have, we now say, a 'psychology'. Moreover, it is a variety of depth psychology. Her characters often do not fully know their own motivations. Thus, we have to deal not only with ironists like Mary Crawford or Henry Tilney who seldom say what they mean, but also with the general run of Austen's characters, who almost always, at least initially (and Emma Woodhouse comes to mind as the most egregious example), are only in imperfect touch with their own minds. Austen's characters will thus not only deliberately mislead their interlocutors, as Henry Crawford does the Bertram girls, but, unknowingly, themselves as well, which the reader must be on his or her guard against.

So by depth psychology I mean the way that Austen's characters usually begin the story in a state of unconsciousness as regards the nature of their desire and its objects. In *Northanger Abbey*, Austen's first novel, the gap between what the heroine thinks she wants, and what she ends up wanting, is perhaps at its widest; in her last, *Persuasion*, perhaps at its narrowest. In our post-Freudian era we are apt to interpret unconsciousness, or depth psychology, in psychoanalytic terms. Austen's interest in unconsciousness is quite different. In *Mansfield Park* Edmund reports to Fanny his farewell speech to Mary Crawford:

> She tried to speak carelessly; but she was not so careless as she wanted to appear. I only said in reply, that from my heart I wished her well, and earnestly hoped that she might soon learn to think more justly, and not owe the most valuable knowledge we could any of us acquire – the knowledge of ourselves and of our duty to the lessons of affliction . . . (*MP* 378)

Austen is not concerned with unconscious drives and their neurotic symptoms, with whatever complex it is that makes Mary 'careless' in spite of her own best self-interest. She is preoccupied, rather, with self-knowledge in a Christian context.[6] As a mainstream Anglican, Austen would have shared the general belief in our fallen, unregenerate nature. As such we are indeed born into 'unconsciousness', into the post-lapsarian state of sin, of being beset, and blinded, by lust, pride, avarice, envy, jealousy, sloth, or anger. For Austen, the self we are to know is marked more by negative than by positive characteristics: to know the self is not to be deceived by worldly ambition or desire. Such self-knowledge, moreover, is a duty, because, until we know ourselves, we cannot know others: and knowing otherness – knowing others, as others, as beings where the lights and shades fall with a certain difference, in ways that command our respect – is the crux of Austen's morality. When we are told that Aunt Norris speaks 'at' rather than to Fanny (MP 267), she stands convicted of immorality: the immorality of denying the otherness of others. Mr Woodhouse is similarly immoral, in that he cannot imagine that others see things differently from the way he does, although this failing is treated in a less harsh – in a generally more comic – fashion.

Austen's religious beliefs render Aunt Norris especially culpable. As an Anglican, Austen was equally distant from Calvinist notions of predestined election and Catholic ones of formalized penance. Salvation, rather, was a matter of continuous personal struggle. Aunt Norris's guilt – like her fictional grotesqueness – lies in the absence of conflict, in the fact that no inner brake is applied to her unregenerate instincts. Austen's heroines are not born good – although they do seem to be born with capabilities others do not have – but are good by dint of perpetual inner struggle. Fanny Price is generally taken to be the most extreme of Austen's paragons, but, even more than Mary Crawford, she suffers from envy, jealousy, and anger. The difference is that she knows she so suffers and accordingly exerts pressure against the warps in her character.

Austen's moral purpose and the achievement of personality in fiction are thus of a piece. Her characters change according to the company they keep because their inner selves are dynamic. And their inner selves are dynamic because there is a tension between what they feel and what they decide to do; between their desires and the moral codes that direct correct action; between self and other. Austen's characters – her personalities – possess the capacity to learn and change as they strive (or learn to strive) to do their duty and know themselves. I said earlier that Austen's characters exist on a continuum between personalities and grotesques. Where they are finally placed on this continuum depends on the degree of conflict they experience: the more conflicted, the more the character tends to the condition of 'personhood'. If we take *Sense and Sensibility*, it is apparent that Marianne is not, at least initially, as fully arrived at personhood as Elinor. This is partly owing to the fact that free indirect speech is used far more sparingly in her case than in Elinor's. We see things much more through Elinor's eyes, and as such we are privy to Elinor's inner conflicts in a way that we are not with Marianne.

As we shall see in a later chapter, Austen's use of free indirect speech is strategically crucial to the entire way in which she structures her narratives, from plot, through theme, to her moral purposes. But for now I want to put this aside and consider the other ways in which, at least initially, Marianne appears less rounded than Elinor. The salient difference is that, when Marianne first appears to us, she labours under the ideological burden of sensibility. *Sense and Sensibility* was conceived, if not finished, in the 1790s, when debates about sensibility touched the nerves of the nation.[7] As a concept, sensibility has its origins in early eighteenth-century moral philosophy. There were two, broad ways of thinking about it, which Chris Jones has helpfully categorized as 'radical' and 'conservative'.[8] Radical sensibility's basic premise is that we are naturally benevolent. According to this view, we have an innate moral sense, where we are instinctively warmed by scenes of virtue and equally disgusted by spectacles of vice. Although there is a strong British tradition of radical sensibility, running from the third Earl of Shaftesbury through Francis Hutcheson to William Godwin, it was principally associated with the nature philosophy of Jean-Jacques Rousseau. The conservative tradition, by contrast, imputed the existence of neither instinctive benevolence nor an innate moral sense. Sensibility, rather, was the instinct to emulate our betters, or our consciousness of how others might view us, both of which instruct us to be better by appealing to our selfish passions. Sensibility was a sensitive topic in the 1790s because it was the conceptual fulcrum for many of the debates about the political and social meaning of the French Revolution. Reformers argued that doing away with things as they are, with the ancient edifice of feudal oppression that lived on in Britain's outmoded institutions, but especially the constitution, would allow mankind's innately benevolent self to stand forth in pristine glory, while their conservative opponents argued that just such a thing had indeed happened across the Channel, with the smashing of the *Ancien Régime* in France, and what burst forth was the very inverse of instinctive benevolence.

Marianne is not a proponent of radical sensibility, but she is a devotee of its fashionable relative, of what I shall call, for the sake of convenience, 'Romantic sensibility', meaning the broad trend towards primitivism in the late eighteenth century, which encompassed, in numerous ways, a turn to nature, including unfenced gardens, the picturesque, the sublime, ballads, the cult of original genius, Evangelicalism in religion, breast feeding, and, for men, long hair instead of wigs, worn naturally rather than powdered.[9] As this list suggests, Romantic sensibility was as much about fashion as it was about politics, but, as Austen well knew, and as any reader of the period would have understood, the two were inextricably linked. For our purposes, the point where the relationship between the two is most knotted was the fashion for romantic love. In the 1790s, romantic love, a sine qua non of Romantic sensibility, was highly politicized. The key issue was primogeniture. Conservatives, such as Edmund Burke, argued for the right of landed families to keep their estates intact through the eldest son on the male line, and, if possible, of aggrandizing them through judicious marriages. Mary Wollstonecraft's radical attack on the practice is worth quoting at length. She addresses Burke in response to his *Reflections on the Revolution in France* (1790):

> The perpetuation of property in our families is one of the privileges you most warmly contend for; but it would not be very difficult to prove that the mind must have a very limited range that thus confines its benevolence to such a narrow circle, which, with great propriety, may be included in the sordid calculations of blind self-love.
>
> A brutal attachment to children has appeared the most conspicuous in parents who have treated them like slaves, and demanded

17

due homage for all the property they transferred to them, during their lives. It has led them to force their children to break the most sacred ties; to do violence to a natural impulse, and run into legal prostitution to increase wealth or shun poverty; and, still worse, the dread of parental malediction has made many weak characters violate truth in the face of Heaven; and, to avoid a father's angry curse, the most sacred promises have been broken.

Who can recount all the unnatural crimes which the laudable, interesting desire of perpetuating a name has produced? The younger children have been sacrificed to the eldest son; sent into exile, or confined in convents, that they might not encroach on what was called, with shameful falsehood, the family estate.[10]

The ills diagnosed by Wollstonecraft, the personal social evils attendant upon children not being allowed to marry for love, or as their own hearts dictate, is recognizably the world of Austen's fiction. Indeed, in so far as Austen's stories ever darken, they do so because tyrannical parents wish to force their children into unsuitable marriages for the sake of their own, selfish aggrandisement. We might think, for instance, of Sir Thomas Bertram hectoring Fanny into marrying Henry Crawford, or, from the other angle, of Mrs Ferrar's interdiction on Edward marrying anybody 'who had not either a great fortune or high rank' (SS 18). Or we might recall Colonel Brandon's tale of the unfortunate Eliza, which could easily furnish Wollstonecraft with matter fit for her moral.

However, Austen's treatment of morals, or politics, is never schematic; she never leaves us with a simple 'either / or'. Sir Thomas comes to regret his treatment of Fanny, comes to regret, even, the selfish and misguided principles on which he had so disastrously instructed his children, while the spontaneous attachments of the heart – the very quick of the ideal of romantic love – is likewise subject to revision and qualification in Austen's fictions. And so it is with Marianne; at the beginning of the novel she is an artless (a self-consciously artless) proponent of Romantic sensibility. As such she can hardly experience inner conflict, as the whole point of sensibility is that one's first instincts – such as one's first romantic attachments – are to be trusted implicitly and completely. Without inner conflict, Marianne drifts dangerously close to the status, if not of a grotesque, then of a comic, or satiric, creation. Thus, at various points, she becomes the sport of the narrator, who makes arch witticisms at Marianne's expense turning on the very predictability of her thoughts and responses, on her determination to live out the life of a Romantic heroine. But that, of course, is not Marianne's fate. Made to suffer through the consequences of her incautiousness and chastened by the image of her selfishness in dwelling excessively on her own jilted misery – reflected back to her in the mirror of Elinor's exemplary behaviour on being similarly disappointed by Edward – she discovers, and changes, and so becomes a personality at last, as she learns to love Colonel Brandon, not by first impulse, but through reflection, or 'sense'.

Self-knowledge (with the implicit assumption that self is difficult or even impossible to know), and 'affliction' (MP 378), as Edmund Bertram puts it, are thus essential aspects of Austen's Anglican view of 'character'; and, out of the dynamism of this mix, there arises the illusion of personality Austen was so expert in creating. However, at this point a distinction needs to be drawn between the broadly Anglican framework within which Austen wrote, and the meaning, if one can so put it, of her characterizations. To accept the truth of the first does not determine the outcome of the second. Austen's basic view of character may be conditioned by Anglican notions of quiet self-improvement, an acknowledgement of sin, a commitment to good works, and a vague expectation of grace, but that is not to say that her personalities are to be explained in Christian terms. Austen does not validate the status quo, whether Anglican, or otherwise. She explores values with a concrete particularity, with the result that she does not leave social values as she found them. It is not a case of being, politically, for or against; certainly not a question of her being apolitical; rather it is that politics and morality are inextricable for her; and morality she explores with a creative subtlety.

In one of the two most significant contemporary reviews of Austen (the other being by Sir Walter Scott), Richard Whateley comments that, although Austen 'has the merit ... of being evidently a Christian writer ... She might defy the most fastidious critic to call any of her novels ... a "dramatic sermon" '.[11] This might sound like the kind of aesthetic point

19

the New Critics were fond of making about how literature was unparaphraseable, was itself experience and not moral information. But Whateley is driving at something different. Whateley argued that 'a new style of novel has arisen, within the last fifteen or twenty years'. Moreover, 'among the authors of this school there is no one superior, if equal, to' Jane Austen.[12] Whateley compares the new school of fiction to 'Flemish painting', by which he means the 'accurate and unexaggerated delineation of events and characters', a 'perfectly correct picture of common life'. This 'minuteness of detail' recalls Austen's celebrated characterization of her writing as 'the little bit (two Inches wide) of Ivory on which I work with so fine a Brush, as produces little effect after much labour'.[13] Austen's apparently self-deprecating remarks have fooled some readers into believing that Austen's art is without substantial ambition, in the manner, say, of a George Eliot, or a Leo Tolstoy, novelists 'of vastly wider and deeper reach'.[14] But Whateley's comments possess a very different tenor. Significantly he contrasts the new novel with romance, meaning, by the latter, works evoking 'splendid scenes of an imaginary world', a 'fairy land' with 'supernatural agents'. Moralists may have been formally exercised by these improbable fictions, but, in reality, such works are far less dangerous than the novel; for, dealing in the self-consciously fictitious, romances cannot confuse the understanding, and so deprave the judgement, of the reader. The novel, by contrast, deals in probabilities, and therein lays both its danger and its promise. Whateley explains why:

> It is a remark [of Aristotle's], that poetry (i.e. narrative, and dramatic poetry) is of a more philosophical character than history; inasmuch as the latter details what has actually happened, of which many parts may chance to be exceptions to the general rules of probability, and consequently illustrate no general principles; whereas the former shews us what must naturally, or would probably, happen under given circumstances; and thus displays to us a comprehensive view of human nature, and furnishes general rules of practical wisdom.[15]

Whateley's defence of the novel is remarkably aggressive. Elsewhere he cites the traditional arguments against fiction, in order to neutralize them. As he says at the beginning of his review, the days of apologizing for the form are over: 'the merits of the best' are 'earnestly discussed by some of the ablest scholars and soundest reasoners of the present day'. The reason for this revolution in taste is the general recognition of the truth of Aristotle's proposition: fiction is more philosophical, more intellectually rigorous, than history. In advancing this view, Whateley sides with an avant garde that, since the 1790s, had been arguing for the merits of a new, sophisticated form of the novel, where probability, and attention to social detail, were philosophically of the essence.[16] Austen's Flemish miniatures, represented, not provincial literalism, but an aesthetic revolution distinguished by fiction's (which is to say, Austen's) ability to imagine the moral life in strenuous, concrete detail, with the whole disciplined by a philosophically conceived 'probability'. Austen's fictions may seem to possess an easy naturalism, but, as Whateley's comments attest, her more sophisticated commentators have realized that the illusion of representational fidelity rested on deep art: hence his crowning encomium, that 'there are few, if any, writers of fiction who have illustrated' Aristotle's aesthetic precepts 'more successfully'.

One might argue that Austen's approach to morality was, effectively, Kantian. Kant had argued that the moral was a mental category; it was, therefore, a matter of understanding and conscious volition. To do the right thing, instinctively, and without thought – such as making space on the 'tube' for a disabled passenger – is not itself a moral act from a Kantian perspective. For such a person to behave morally, she would have had to overcome her desire to remain seated; to have reasoned that a person with only one good leg had a better right to a seat than a person with two; and then, and only then, to have risen, and with the best grace she could muster, offer it to the disabled passenger. Austen, too, sees morality in conscious rather than unconscious acts. To put it another way, Austen is not interested in characters that instinctively do the right thing; she is interested, rather, in those who struggle towards correct action, in characters for whom morality is an education.

But, as Richard Rorty has pointed out, she is also a Kantian in another, very important respect. As just mentioned, doing one's duty, unthinkingly, is to avoid one's moral responsibilities. For Kant, morality can never be coded as a series of rights and wrongs; instead, each case must be taken on its merits and reasoned through. Such an attitude to morality admits the contingent, the concrete particularity that subtly makes one case different from another. In Kantian ethics, it is incumbent upon the philosopher to ask, what, in a given situation, with this or that unique particularity, is the right thing to do? Rorty argues that, if this kind of ethical enquiry is not as vigorous as it once was, it is weak not because of any philosophical deficiencies on its part, but because it has been supplanted by the novel. According to Rorty, the subjunctive spirit of Kant's ethical project (if one were ... what ought one do?) is performed much better by the novel, precisely because the novel's exemplary representations are far more concrete and detailed than any test case a philosopher might dream up. The novel imagines the social realities, which ultimately must condition Kant's ethical suppositions, more thoroughly than philosophical speculation invites. According to Rorty, it is in the work of Jane Austen that the novel comes into its own as a form capable of refining upon Kant's ethics, an assessment surprisingly congruent with Whateley's contemporary one.[17] It is not simply the case that Austen imagines more hypothetical situations in greater detail than a Kantian moral philosopher might do. The difference, rather, is in the quality of the imagining. But wherein lies this qualitative difference in Austen?

I want to sketch out an answer by referring to an essay written over fifty years ago by Lionel Trilling, entitled 'Manners, Morals, and the Novel'. Trilling argued that, as far as novelists are concerned, 'manners make men'.[18] By 'manners' Trilling meant that elusive category of cultural differences by which we know someone is from one county rather another, or a member of one class rather than another. It encompasses differences in the way people talk, dress, and consume. As far as the novelist is concerned, manners really signify only when there is contrast, for the effect of such difference is to throw manners into 'observable relief as the living representation' of ideas and ideals. Thus, for Trilling, the real basis of the novel is 'a tension between a middle class and an aristocracy'.[19] For instance, consider the famous speech in *Pride and Prejudice* where Lady Catherine de Bourgh, Darcy's Aunt, remonstrates with Elizabeth Bennet for so forgetting herself as to imagine that the she might marry a man so far superior to her in rank as Mr Darcy. Elizabeth responds that Mr. Darcy 'is a gentleman; I am a gentleman's daughter; so far we are equal' (*PP* 287). Elizabeth is, of course, being provocatively disingenuous, for there are manifest differences between them. Elizabeth's father's tenure as a member of the landed gentry is extremely tenuous, comprising a relatively modest estate entailed away from his male-less family. Moreover, her mother's relatives, the Gardiners, connect her directly to the city, to trade, and to the 'middle classes'. Darcy's very large estate, with its renowned house and gardens, links him upwards towards the aristocratic grandees, an upward trajectory marked by his connection to his titled aunt, Lady Catherine de Bourgh (a name signalling that she comes by her title through birth, and not marriage; if Elizabeth is a gentleman's daughter, Lady Catherine is an aristocrat's).[20] As far as a tension between the middle class and the aristocracy is concerned, one may say that, in the confrontation between Elizabeth and Lady Catherine, the air crackles. In making her provocative statement, Elizabeth is not denying the obvious material realities that separate her and Darcy. But she is questioning what it means to be a 'gentleman'. Or rather, in an aggressive fashion she is asserting the view of many members of the provincial middling classes – of the country gentry, and those who make their living among them – that the epithet 'gentle' signifies a body of values, an 'ideology', as Trilling would put it, of which membership is a matter of moral striving, not a simple question of birth, or rank, and certainly not a matter of vulgar cash. It is an animus that pervades much 'middle-class' literature, of a certain kind, and that has as its object the criticism of the unreformed upper classes who imperil the country through their moral laxness, their conspicuous consumption, and the dereliction of the duties that come with their class privileges (an animus that finds its clearest expression, in Austen's works, in the depiction of Sir Walter Elliot, in *Persuasion*). Although she employs the language of birth (she is a 'gentleman's daughter'), Elizabeth Bennet really means the language of personal merit;

it is because she is secure in her countervailing ideology that she is able to withstand Lady de Bourgh's onslaught, effectively putting the latter in her place, as someone whose manners place her rather below, than above, Elizabeth. Through class tension, then, manners are thrown into observable relief as the embodiment of ideas and ideals. Everything about Elizabeth – the way she talks, dresses, moves – bespeaks the class, or rather 'rank', and the values to which she consciously, and unconsciously, belongs; while the same may be said of Lady Catherine, or Darcy, for that matter. When Trilling says that, for the novelist, manners make men, he means these innumerable cultural signifiers that constitute a shorthand for the construction of character, for character in the novel first and foremost arises out of social stereotypes. Thus in the Hollywood film *Clueless*, based on *Emma*, the heroine is recast as an LA 'valley girl', a social stereotype that will immediately help the viewer place the character, not simply in terms of what such a character is likely to be like, but in terms of the values she will hold, as regards, say, sex, shopping, and clothes. If such references are vivid, and immediately comprehensible to contemporary audiences, especially to those with a knowledge of the San Fernando valley, so, too, were the references with which Austen veils the character of Elizabeth Bennet, or any other of her heroines, for her contemporary audiences.

But, as we have seen, Austen's characters – her personalities – never remain stereotypes for long. They change, which is to say they defeat, and challenge, the expectations Austen's characterizations initially invite. Emma Woodhouse, we are told, is 'handsome, clever, and rich' (*E*. 7). The language is Emma's, and as such it invites a certain amount of type casting, of Emma as a complacent, self-satisfied, wealthy Home Counties girl. If Emma is rich throughout, at least materially, there are periods when she appears as neither handsome nor clever. In the end, she eventually learns to deserve her own epithets, but only by undergoing a process that redefines what these things might be, so that they are transmuted into a quite different triplet, one she eventually learns to apply favourably to her rival, Jane Fairfax: 'Birth, abilities, and education' (*E*. 345).

Manners make men, and not simply as type casting. Manners, rather, are the semiological medium through which we socially know others and even ourselves. As such they are a site of change, interrogation, and revision. For it is not only the reader who must adjust her first impressions of what a character's manners might portend; so, too, do the characters within the story. If we know characters – others – first through their manners, so do Austen's personalities. Just as we go through a process of reading, of getting to know, Elizabeth Bennet, so does Elizabeth Bennet go through a similar process with Mr Darcy. Elizabeth Bennet is not just a representative of a certain set of country, middle-class values: she also views the world through them. And, through the medium of her values, Darcy, crudely (and the crudeness is as much on her side as it is on his), appears as a stereotypically proud member of the upper gentry, as someone not at all to Elizabeth's tastes. Elizabeth not only learns to love Darcy; she learns to be fair to him, to view him in a more accurate, and less stereotypical, light.

The reader's task, in reading Jane Austen, is thus a large one. She must not only form an opinion of the characters Austen presents to her; but she must assess, must judge and weigh, Austen's characters doing precisely the same thing to each other, for that is often how we know other characters in Austen: through the medium of the heroine's perceptions. In Elizabeth Bennet's assessment of Mr Darcy, and Darcy's of Miss Bennet, where, exactly, lie the rights and the wrongs? Not only as the characters see them, but also as Austen herself does, and beyond Austen, the reader, which is where the moral buck finally stops. Hence Trilling's appraisal of the European novel – an appraisal shared, as we have seen, by Richard Rorty – as the 'finest', meaning the most particular, form of ethical enquiry yet devised by Western culture. Particular, because it is 'concrete', meaning mediated through the social realities elusively embodied by manners.

However, it is not quite so simple as that. Or rather it is not so simple as Trilling's representation of manners sometimes suggests. Trilling sees manners as the elusive embodiment of class-based values, and therefore as a means of thinking through ideological conflict in socially nuanced ways. As such

Trilling appears to restrict his pool of semiological material to aspects of behaviour, speech, and dress. But, as we have seen in the case of Marianne and 'sensibility', the pool of semiological material on which the novelist draws is actually much larger and more complex. The fashionable affectations of sensibility are certainly an aspect of Marianne's manners, and the manners of the period; but they also imply a body of values that exist purely discursively, as a body of texts, about other texts. Marianne's 'sensibility' mobilizes references to Rousseau, to Mackenzie's *The Man of Feeling*, and the whole body of sensibility fiction;[21] to landscape theory;[22] to political economy and moral philosophy.[23] Similarly, in *Northanger Abbey*, complex references are made to the Gothic genre and debates about literary and political 'terror'; in *Mansfield Park*, to the reception of German literature and the Abolitionist movement; while throughout Austen's major novels references to the politically inflected debates about landscape improvement form a running theme. In other words, Austen's novels are 'concrete', because they are also abstract. In creating a complex cultural semiology through which her characters live and move, Austen is amazingly inclusive. Her generic range may be narrow, but, within that range, her references are broad and densely packed.

When Richard Whateley argues that Jane Austen adopts a philosophically sophisticated stance towards probability, he does not simply mean that she has a particularly fine sense of what might happen next, or a horror of obvious coincidence. He means, rather, that Austen, in a fashion never before attained in the novel, represents her characters as caught in the web and woof of social complexity, in conflicts where characters see each other through the medium of ideologically tinged 'manners', and where changing according to the company one keeps involves the hunches one derives from a complex, semiologically dense, social network.

I think we can discount the claim that Austen's purpose was to produce the illusion of personality. In so far as we can know it, her intention was to create 'probable' fictions. The word and its cognates recur repeatedly in Austen's letters, as a mark of her intent and difference.[24] The word was a cliché of contemporary criticism, and we might therefore discount its importance on the grounds that it was a non-signifying platitude.[25] The value of Richard Whatley's review is that it spells out the philosophical project contemporaneously attached to it. In understanding Austen's achievement of personality historically we must begin with this philosophical project. However, as the same time we must stand back from it and regard it critically. Here, again, Trilling's thesis requires some amendment. The act of privileging manners, as the medium through which we know the human subject, is itself a political or ideological stance. Here is Edmund Burke extolling the importance of manners in the very heat of polemical battle over the meaning of the French Revolution:

> manners are of more importance than laws. Upon them, in a great measure, the laws depend. The law touches us but here and there, and now and then. Manners are what vex or soothe, corrupt or purify, exalt or debase, barbarise or refine us ... They give their whole form and colour to our lives. According to their quality, they aid morals, they supply them, or they totally destroy them.[26]

Burke argues that society is best reformed through patterns of good conduct embedded in the culture – through 'manners' – rather than through abstract principles or laws (which do not 'touch us'). Manners are thus not a value-free medium through which we know 'men' or articulate ideas and ideals: they are, in themselves, a political ideology, with a history. The act of writing in the genre of the novel of manners is already to accept that the self is how history has made it, which is why writers with strong antipathies to the British class structure, such as the Brontës, Hardy, or Lawrence, have been hostile to the form, an hostility shared by American romancers, such as Nathaniel Hawthorne and Herman Melville.[27] Austen's project of fictional probability (so necessary to her art of creating 'personality') was thus not only philosophical, but political.

2

Genre

Like all major writers, Austen changed the genre in which she wrote. Indeed, in the view of her twentieth-century critics, she is the key figure in the early nineteenth-century consolidation of the novel.[1] Her contemporaries may have believed that the future belonged to Sir Walter Scott and the historical romance, to what Scott himself called, with becoming self-deprecation, 'the big bow-wow',[2] but we know now that it was really in possession of the Home Counties ironist with her vivid depictions of late Georgian, country, social life. Or rather we do, if we are charting the forward progress of the English novel, from George Eliot through Henry James, to Elizabeth Bowen, Barbara Pym, and Henry Green, or, in our own day, to Martin Amis, Ian McEwan, and Jane Rogers. In other words, Austen represented the future if we think of the novel as a form that attempts to sound character as realized in and through a highly particularized social reality.

But that is only one strand of the 'novel', a strand some have perceived as peculiarly, if not uniquely, English.[3] For example, a number of American writers found Austen a problem. James Fenimore Cooper notoriously claimed that he first tried novel writing on the grounds that he could do no worse than Jane Austen; moreover, he quickly dropped her style of novel, opting instead for the more 'masculine' historical romance of Sir Walter Scott, which Cooper naturalized as the Leatherstocking novels.[4] Mark Twain frequently made her the butt of his jokes, claiming, for instance, that a ship's library without any Jane Austen would 'make a fairly good library out of a library that hadn't a book in it'.[5] More recently, the Mexican novelist Carlos Fuentes asserted that, in order to write, he had to expunge from his mind all vestiges of the claustrophobic spaces of Austen's middle-class salons, if he was to say anything at all meaningful about Mexican realities. Nor is this hostility confined to foreign traditions of the novel. Angela Carter and Salman Rushdie both very self-consciously looked above, and beyond, Austen and her literary progeny, finding inspiration elsewhere, such as South American 'Magic Realism', a movement not unlike Charlotte Brontë's angry rejection of Austen's cloistered realism in favour of the open spaces of romance.[6]

If the novel today has many strands, so did it in the 1790s, when Austen first sat down to write. Perhaps the most persistent fracture in the history of the novel is that between 'novel' and 'romance'. By 'novel' Austen's contemporaries generally meant a probable depiction of contemporary manners, such as Austen provides us, whereas 'romance' signified an improbable tale, generally set in past times, and often featuring chivalry and/or the supernatural. Two of Austen's early works, *Northanger Abbey* and *Sense and Sensibility*, burlesque romance conventions, the former more systematically than the latter, as if in settling down into the novel Austen had first to square her accounts with romance. Another way of putting it was that she was making shrewd decisions as an aspirant professional writer. As Peter Garside and James Raven pointed out in their introductions to *The English Novel 1770–1829*, works bearing the description 'romance' or 'tale' in their title pages were sharply on the decline in the early 1800s, as was the particular fashion for the Gothic.[7] As the Irish writer Charles Maturin observed ruefully in 1818, the Gothic style of writing was 'already out' by 1807.[8] The publication of *Waverley* in 1814 was to reinvigorate the romance form by cleansing it of its absurdities, co-opting the novel's realistic techniques, and particularizing the past as 'history'. Scott did not use the past as mere scenery but employed actual events as a background to the action with a view to the significant historical lessons to be drawn, in this way bringing the kudos of history painting to fiction. Austen wrote in the interregnum between two high points of 'romance' – between Ann Radcliffe's last work in 1797 and Sir Walter Scott's first one in 1814, between *The Italian* and *Waverley* – when the 'novel' was in vogue, and during a period when women dominated the marketplace for fiction, achieving a 'market share' in 1813 of 66 per cent of the new novels published.[9]

One could say that Austen was following fashion in being a writer who preferred the novel over romance, or that she was simply being professional and practical. Neither comment is particularly helpful in so far as both obscure the fundamental truth about Austen's use of genre. The novel has always been a hybrid form, a mix of many pre-existing genres: Austen takes full advantage of this hybridity. In a letter to the Prince Regent's secretary, James Stanier Clarke (1 April 1816), Austen diplomatically responds:

> You are very very kind in your hints as to the sort of composition which might recommend me at present, and I am fully sensible that an historical romance, founded on the House of Saxe Coburg, might be much more to the purpose or profit or popularity than such pictures of domestic life in country villages as I deal in. But I could no more write a romance than an epic poem. I could not sit seriously down to write a serious romance under any other motive than to save my life.[10]

The Prince Regent had it let be known to Austen that he was an admirer, and that she had his permission to dedicate her next novel (*Emma*) to him. It was an offer she could not refuse. In the follow-up correspondence, Clarke had hinted that a historical romance of the royal family would be a welcome addition to her œuvre. Austen, who in an earlier letter had confided that she 'hated' the Regent, was certainly unlikely to comply, and she is doubtless being honest when she intimates that a pistol held to her head would be about the only means of bringing her to write hagiography. But her comments are misleading if we interpret them as meaning that she writes a generically simple style of country novel. On the contrary, her narratives are generically complex. Trying to compass them in a phrase is to find oneself referring, laboriously, to her 'romantic-pastoral-comedies', or her 'comic *Bildungsroman* of manners'. Austen's fictions may look seamless to us now, as natural, organic expressions of what a 'novel' should be, but peer at them closely, and what emerges is something of a Frankenstein's monster, a form stitched together from numer-

30

ous, scavenged sources. Indeed, this is so much so in the case of *Northanger Abbey* that critics at one time bickered about whether it really was, after all, a novel.[11] In this chapter I shall briefly review the different generic elements that go to compose an Austen novel, dwelling on those instances where Austen is most innovative. At the same time I enlarge on the ideological meanings inherent in her use of manners, as introduced in the previous chapter.

THE COMIC PLOT

The most obvious aspect of Austen's novels is that they are comedies, and before they were novels, comedies were plays. Northrop Frye describes the 'formula' used by Austen, and which comes down to us from Greek New Comedy:

> What normally happens is that a young man wants to marry a young woman, that his desire is resisted by some opposition, usually paternal, and that near the end of the play some twist in the plot enables the hero to have his will. In this simple pattern there are several complex elements. In the first place, the movement of comedy is usually a movement from one kind of society to another. At the beginning of the play the obstructing characters are in charge of the play's society, and the audience recognizes that they are usurpers. At the end of the play the device in the plot that brings the hero and heroine together causes a new society to crystallize around the hero, and the moment when this crystallization occurs is the point of resolution in the action, the comic discovery, *anagnorisis* or *cognito*.[12]

Thematically, stymied love represents social disharmony; the marriage with which the play ends accordingly restores the social order to what it should be. Austen's six major novels are all variations on this pattern.

In a major intervention on *Hamlet*, William Empson argued that debates about Hamlet's existential indecisiveness were completely beside the point. Coming near the end of the vogue for Revenge tragedies, Shakespeare had to deal with a situation in which the audience knew that the play was going to end badly, in slaughter; the trick was to keep the revenger on stage in ways that kept the audience interested, and guessing, while arranging the predictable denouement with a surprising swiftness.[13] Austen is equally resourceful in finding novel ways of prolonging the inevitable marriage, while complicating the meaning – the thematic richness – of her comic plots. *Northanger Abbey* and *Sense and Sensibility*, both early novels, include obvious examples of paternal (or, indeed, of maternal) opposition. Her later novels are more subtle and resourceful. For instance, in *Emma* the obstacles are entirely located within the heroine herself. Everyone, and everything, points to her marriage to Mr Knightley. It is the most satisfactory of all possible marital outcomes for her father; it is welcomed by her friends; by the community, whose cohesion is cemented by the union; and, of course, by Mr Knightley, and by Emma herself, if only she would know it. But she does not know it, owing to a profound lack of self-knowledge. And not knowing herself, she does not know others, hence her dismal record in predicting marriages. Having hit upon the perfectly obvious union of Miss Taylor and Mr Weston, Emma prides herself, quite erroneously, on her powers of marital foresight, whereupon there follows a highly mortifying comedy of errors. Emma fails to see that she, and not Harriet Smith, is Mr Elton's true object. Her complacent belief in her powers of romantic divination blinds her to the courtship of Frank Churchill and Jane Fairfax occurring under her nose. At one point she even believes Mr Knightley and Harriet are an item, having been previously disabused of her notion that Frank Churchill was Harriet's object. Finally, in interfering with the natural love affair between Harriet and Robert Martin, she threatens to do real harm to the harmony of the community by preventing a match she ought to promote. Indeed, as far as maintaining and nurturing the idyllic social order of Highbury is concerned – a community of such neighbourliness that indigent spinsters thrive owing to the tactful generosity of their neighbours – Emma is its most disruptive and dangerous element, mainly because she does not know where she, and her love, properly belong. This internalization of the obstacle to marriage within the heroine herself is in one respect a complete inversion of the comic plot. In another it is just a very clever refinement of it. Emma is dangerous, not just because of who she is (handsome, clever, and rich) but because of her nurture. In abdicating his role as a strong moral lead, Mr Woodhouse has left Emma to imbibe an incorrect way of thinking from her society at large, but especially through novels, from which she derives her propensity for romantic intrigue and scandal. Fundamentally, Emma is a snob, which is to say she has an incorrect idea of class distinctions, or, in terms the novel itself uses, of 'rank', and what is owing to it. It is this snobbishness that threatens Highbury's 'organic' unity, where 'organic' is a construct of the conservative ideology *Emma*, with reservations, endorses. Mr Knightley, on the other hand, has a just appreciation of rank. To put it another way, he is the idealized embodiment of country, Tory values, where the landed families enjoy the highest status while also bearing the greatest obligations, and where the corrupting example of the great, Whig aristocrats is conveniently absent. Mr Knightley quietly works for the benefit of the community, whether endeavouring to promote the welfare and happiness of his tenant farmers, the Martins (from matters of farming improvement to marriage), to ensuring the Bateses are well supplied with apples and carriage rides, to easing the social way for new money, for wealthy trading families such as the Coles. For Tory thinkers, the proper answer to the French Revolutionary turmoil was the regeneration of the unique qualities of the English social order, best represented in the country, where gradations between ranks were many, therefore slight, and permeable. In such a community, where all knew their social duty, charity was such that no family fell into incendiary poverty, while a proper respect for merit ensured that rising commercial talent was seamlessly absorbed into the social order, when deserving, thus preventing class resentments.

To begin with, Emma has only an imperfect understanding of this ideology, and as a result is apt to interpret it according to the letter rather than, as Knightley does, its spirit. As such Emma is a repository of dangerous social and political values. Through her afflictions, her mortifying acts of romantic misprision, her 'penance' (*E.* 152), she is gradually led to a right way of thinking and to a knowledge of her own mind and heart. In the end, not only she, but the community, are much the better for it as proper order is, not so much restored, as nurtured and maintained.

33

In *Emma*, the thematically disruptive opposition of the father is internalized within the daughter, where the father's weakness becomes the daughter's headlong rush into error. *Mansfield Park* is the complete reverse of this structure. Fanny Price knows her own mind, and whom she wants to marry, virtually from the beginning. Fanny not only knows who she wants to marry: she knows who to marry for the greatest benefit of the community. But, owing to the disparity of station between her and Edmund, initially, no one else wishes it, including Edmund. Opposition to the marriage is thus conventionally located in the father, in Sir Thomas Bertram, only not steadily so, for he, too, is a man of principle, and therefore susceptible to moral persuasion. The incorrigible literalist in class affairs is Mrs Norris, who comes to figure as a kind of scapegoat, as the repository of damaging, overly rigid social attitudes, which the novel repudiates in a manner calculated to appeal to the reader's sense of malicious pleasure. If in *Emma* the learning curve is experienced by the heroine, in *Mansfield Park* it is country society at large, as represented by the community of Mansfield, who have to learn the true desirableness of the marriage between Fanny and Edmund, a union of merit rather than of rank or fortune, a lesson they learn through the hard lessons inflicted by the worldly, morally chaotic, Crawfords. In *Pride and Prejudice* the obstacles are divided between the primary couple as they initially make love with the baggage of class differences interposing between them. Lady Catherine de Bourgh's opposition is in the end relegated to the past, as an expression of outmoded attitudes to rank and station. Differences in rank divide the lovers in *Persuasion*, as they do in all of Austen's novels, bar *Emma*, where the disparity is only slight, but in her last novel Austen detaches the obstacle, or interdiction, from any association with a particular character, transforming it instead into an abstract duty. Although urged by the otherwise admirable Lady Russell (her father being morally nugatory), Anne Elliot initially sacrifices Wentworth on a matter of principle; in other words, not to the actual opposition of her family, but to the idea of it. As such, *Persuasion* may be said to have become self-reflexive about its own generic, comedic, origins.

In the two 'early' novels we see more of the conventional figure of the father as paternal ogre. *Sense and Sensibility* skirts narrative cliché, or romance, partly by introducing the stock figure of the seducer, in the shape of Willoughby, and partly through an unreasoning, opposing parent. However, rather than a man, the tyrant in question is the absurdly irrational Mrs Ferrars. Colonel Brandon's story of Eliza arguably does not skirt cliché at all, but embraces it. Eliza's progress, from Colonel's Brandon's childhood sweetheart, to the enforced bride of the Colonel's brother, to adulteress, to tubercular beggar (and presumed prostitute) is effectively the story Austen parodies as cliché in *Pride and Prejudice*, through Mary's sententious comments on the lessons afforded by Lydia's conduct: 'that loss of virtue in a female is irretrievable – that one false step involves her in endless ruin – that her reputation is no less brittle than it is beautiful' (*PP* 234).[14] Eliza's story, however, is only a brief inset tale. Only *Northanger Abbey* employs the typical figure of the tyrannical father to forward its plot, but even here, as one would expect, Austen inverts the convention. Rather than scheming to keep the lovers apart, General Tilney connives to bring them together, only throwing Catherine out on her ear when he learns of her poverty. Even then he proves to be, not an implacable blackguard, a 'Montoni', as Catherine Morland calls him, referring to the antagonist of Ann Radcliffe's *The Mysteries of Udolpho*, a feudal tyrant who will stop at nothing to enlarge his property, but only an upper-class boor who is brought round by time, a rosier picture of Catherine's finances, and his son's stubbornness.

A question we might fairly ask is why did Austen stick to comedies? Why, in her novels, did she never move in a more tragic direction? This is a question we can never properly answer, and, if we could, the solution might very well be the banal observation that hers was a comic genius. However, I think it worth dwelling on, if only for a moment, as it helps us see the generic possibilities Austen's writing butts up against. Given her 'given', her concern with marriage plots, to darken her canvas would have involved her, inevitably, in the Gothic. A tyrannical father in conflict with his daughter over her marriage choice is one of the Gothic genre's most salient features. Whereas he commands her to marry in the interests of 'alliance', she struggles to marry for love. As we have already seen in Mary Wollstonecraft's rebuke to Edmund

Burke for supporting primogeniture, such patriarchal tyranny was generally regarded, by those of a liberal disposition, as a 'feudal' remnant, a regressive social habit of the more unprincipled aristocracy. In trying to achieve something new, and fresh, Austen, perforce, would have had to avoid the Gothic's hackneyed plots, where paternal opposition would be impossible to represent without appearing to be 'unnatural and overdrawn', to borrow Mr Allen's terms of critical disapprobation (NA 157). Such plots would also have moved her closer to dissenting opinion. Austen's solution to the problem is to avoid paternal tyranny altogether (Emma); to burlesque it (Northanger Abbey); to inject 'matriarchal' opposition instead (Sense and Sensibility, Pride and Prejudice); or to embody opposition in a principle, rather than a figure, leaving her free to represent the father as a buffoon, rather than an ogre (Persuasion). It is noticeable, however, that Austen's works with the most sombre tone are those that stress the difficulties young women face in a society where kinship practices are a mainstay of the patriarchal order.[15] Where these difficulties obtrude with a potentially tragic force, in, that is, Mansfield Park and Persuasion, the paternal figures do indeed cross over into Gothic territory. Sir Walter Elliott's moral monstrosity is neutralized through regularly applied doses of ridicule. Mansfield Park is another matter.

In his initial rage at Fanny's refusal of Henry Crawford, a very different Sir Thomas suddenly appears from behind his customary mask of stern benevolence, an appearance we might call 'Gothic', as long as we understand Gothic as a shorthand for social antagonisms embedded deep within late Enlightenment culture. The contours of Sir Thomas's mounting anger are worth dwelling on. Much to Sir Thomas's surprise and gratification, Henry Crawford has approached him for Fanny's hand in marriage; to his equal chagrin, Fanny has refused the offer. Sir Thomas is intent on getting to the bottom of her incomprehensible refusal. Fanny has just told him that Henry Crawford's attentions 'were always – what I did not like':

> Sir Thomas looked at her with deeper surprise. 'This is beyond me ... This requires explanation. Young as you are, and having seen scarcely anyone, it is hardly possible that your affections——'

He paused and eyed her fixedly. He saw her lips formed into a *no*, though the sound was inarticulate, but her face was like scarlet. That, however, in so modest a girl might be very compatible with innocence; and chusing at least to appear satisfied, he quickly added, 'No, no, I know *that* is quite out of the question . . .' (*MP* 261)

As I mentioned before, Austen is attentive, not just to manners, but to the ideological structures in which manners inhere. Fanny's unvoiced 'no' is just such an instance. It dawns on Sir Thomas that Fanny's affections, her desires, might already be engaged. The scene, and Sir Thomas's response, are in fact highly complex. The first layer we need to uncover concerns the cultural status of female desire at this time. 'Female desire' was constructed, and regulated, through medical and ethical discourses. According to the dictates of sensibility – according to what we might call the discourse of modesty – women were both invested with sexual desire and prohibited from voicing it. In this respect J. J. Rousseau's *Emile* is an exemplary text. According to Rousseau, it is appropriate and natural for men to express their desires through language, but modesty prohibits it for women. For Rousseau, women express their desires through the language of the body, through blushes, sighs, or quick breathing.[16] I shall come back to this point in the next chapter, as Austen frequently engages with this restrictive construction of the feminine; for now, I want to concentrate on the tact of Austen's representation. Under Sir Thomas's fixed, masculine gaze, Fanny apparently falls into line with Rousseau's stereotype. Fanny's affections have been engaged: she desires Edmund. Words fail her. She cannot muster a lying 'no', but her body betrays her: 'her face was like scarlet'. Austen then switches into free indirect speech. Sir Thomas considers that her blush signifies female innocence; or, rather, he chooses to so interpret it. According to the view Sir Thomas takes of her, Fanny blushes, not because she desires, but because desire itself is prohibited by her natural innocence, or modesty. As an innocent, Fanny must blush at the very mention of desire. In effect, we witness Sir Thomas construing Fanny in such a way that she conforms with his understanding of gender norms. 'Modest' now assumes a double meaning: it refers to Sir Thomas's assessment of Fanny (what we might call modesty's common sense or familiar meaning) but it also signifies the social values that oppress Fanny (modesty as ideological invention). Clearly, Fanny does not conform to Sir Thomas's (or Rousseau's) 'modest'. Fanny may be said to fail to aspirate her 'no', not because language is the inappropriate medium of female desire, but because to say it would be a lie. The reader is free to speculate that Fanny might very well voice her desire, given different circumstances, and that she blushes, not because she is reminded of her desire for Edmund, but because she is embarrassed about fibbing. Behind Sir Thomas's simplistic construction of Fanny the reader is invited to spy a more complex being.

If Fanny stands for romantic love, Sir Thomas represents patriarchy of a certain, old-fashioned kind. The difference between them encapsulates an ideological rift that was one of the many fault lines that divided public opinion during the early years of the French Revolution. Progressive opinion supported the individual against the dictates of the family. Just as radicals supported the rights of man, in general, so they supported the rights of woman, in particular, to choose in what was one of the most significant affairs of her life. One might characterize this difference as the tension between an aristocratic attitude towards love and marriage, where primogeniture and the discipline of maintaining the estate take precedence, and a middle-class one in which individual desire is more important, given that class's relative lack of accumulated capital. The French philosopher and social historian Michel Foucault has described this conflict as between a 'deployment of alliance' and a 'deployment of sexuality'.[17] By the first phrase Foucault means the way in which the disciplines of primogeniture were institutionalized as legal and social practices, as the means of perpetuating aristocratic power; by the second, he means how the nineteenth-century obsession with sex conceals a countervailing, bourgeois will to power. Sexuality was medicalized, manufactured, and controlled, even as its sites proliferated within society. If 'blood' was the totemic value of aristocracy, for the bourgeoisie, it was 'health'.

This tension, or rift, in the body politic is the territory of the Gothic. As mentioned a moment ago, the most common *mise en scène* of the 1790s Gothic is the conflict between female desire and family convenience, a daughter whose love object contravenes the dictates of alliance and a father who is determined to enforce them. Radcliffe's *A Sicilian Romance* provides the clearest expression of this ritualized conflict, although one might also think of Coleridge's *Christabel*, where intimations of his daughter's sexuality send Sir Leoline into a chivalrous rage. In *Mansfield Park*, we appear to be heading down this road, as Sir Thomas works himself into a kind of controlled, paternal hysteria at Fanny's recalcitrance. His address to Fanny touches on all aspects of the generational, ideological, and discursive conflict I have been sketching:

> 'I had thought you peculiarly free from wilfulness of temper, self-conceit, and every tendency to that independence of spirit, which prevails so much in modern days, even in young women, and which in young women is offensive and disgusting beyond all common offence. But you have now shown me that you can be wilful and perverse, that you can and will decide for yourself, without any consideration or deference for those who have surely some right to guide you . . . The advantage or disadvantage of your family – of your parents – your brothers and sisters – never seems to have had a moment's share in your thoughts on this occasion. How *they* might be benefited, how *they* must rejoice in such an establishment for you – is nothing to *you*.' (*MP* 263)

In her adaptation of *Mansfield Park*, Patricia Rozema clearly sees the Gothic potential of this moment, as she has Harold Pinter play the scene, as Sir Thomas, with a kind of Coleridgean fury. Austen herself pulls back from exaggerated paternal beastliness: 'He ceased. Fanny was by this time crying so bitterly, that angry as he was, he would not press that article farther' (*MP* 263). There is a limit to how far Austen will take monstrous paternalism. And yet there is another edge to this scene. A moment ago I quoted how, skipping over the thought that Fanny's heart might be engaged, Sir Thomas chooses to appear satisfied that she is 'innocent'. The delicate phrasing of this act of free indirect speech invites the reader to entertain the contrary possibility: that Sir Thomas suspects that she is not innocent, that her heart is engaged, and, if so, then necessarily with someone close to her, such as Edmund. If so, we have another possible source for Sir Thomas's rage: the family he is thinking of, as being defrauded by Fanny's perversity, is his own, through Edmund's entrapment to a portionless relative, a possibility that would rather heighten than lower Sir Thomas's Gothic lights, especially as it reveals him as wielding the construct of innocence, or modesty, as a weapon against Fanny. As he uses the phase, the 'innocence' he attributes to Fanny would mean, not just amorous propriety, but a reduced level of marital expectation.

I started this investigation into Sir Thomas's behaviour by saying that veering out of the path of comedy presented Austen with peculiar difficulties. Having her heroines run tragically afoul of the law of the father takes Austen into an area of fictional crudity, of the overdrawn, where she clearly cannot go; but it also takes her into radical territory. As Gary Kelly helpfully reminds us, Tory ideology was perfectly content with contemplating reform of the patriarchal order;[18] but any such fictional treatment of reform automatically became entangled in the discursive strands of the Gothic, which tended to support Wollstonecraft's equation of paternal tyranny over marriage with a fundamental dysfunction of a class-bound patriarchal order. In such a situation, it would have been impossible to keep a Tory critique in quarantine from a Radical one. On the other hand, Austen is clearly sensible of restrictive, patriarchal, kinship practices in her society, which not only curtailed a woman's sphere of action, but rendered her legally insecure, once married, as regards her rights to property, her children, and even her person.[19] I have dwelt on this question at such length, as debates about the degree of Austen's transgression, or conformity, frequently turn on the degree of Austen's hostility to the patriarchal order. By considering Austen's contemporary, generic choices, it seems to me that we draw some useful information, as her plots skirt, and draw away from – in fact always move within the shadow of – a darkening consciousness of the social meaning of the 'Gothic' father.

THE LEARNING CURVE

As mentioned in the previous section, and the previous chapter, a process of education is a recurring formal compo-

nent of an Austen novel. Such a process is now so integral to
the novel form it is possible to forget that it was not always so.
For example, it is arguable that neither Tom Jones nor Pamela
knows anything more at the finish of their adventures, their
misfortunes and trials, than they do at the beginning. They
represent, rather, the triumph of certain qualities over adver-
sity: a generous, open manliness in Tom's case, and an
incorruptible attachment to her morality in Pamela's. Austen
did not invent the novel of education, or what the Germans
refer to as the *Bildungsroman*, meaning, literally, a novel of
'pictures', or scenes, depicting the salient stages in the hero's
development. However, she did bring the device of moral
education to a new level of sophistication within the English
novel. One of her innovations was to adapt the narrative
structure of tragedy to her comic plots. As Aristotle tells us, in
classical Greek tragedies the forward movement of the narrative is arrested by moments of recognition or discovery
(*anagnorisis* or *cognitio*, to use the terms we earlier encountered
in Northrop Frye's description of Classical comic structures).
Aristotle goes on to say that the 'most effective form of
discovery is that which is accompanied by reversals . . .'.[20]

To take the obvious example of *Oedipus Rex* (as Aristotle
himself does), the upward curve of Oedipus' fortune is halted
by the king's recognition of his responsibility for Thebes'
afflictions (it being brought home to him that he has killed his
father and married his mother), a moment of recognition
followed by a fairly swift reversal of fortune, as Oedipus
quickly renders himself, through the extremity of his own
horror, an eyeless, beggarly outcast. Austen adapts this structure to the comic mode, complicating it as she does so by
disjoining 'reversals' from 'recognitions'. Thus readers have
often been led into error when analysing *Northanger Abbey*, by
supposing that Henry Tilney's speech to Catherine Morland
about England's progressive civil qualities (a neighbourhood
of voluntary spies making wife-murder difficult) is Catherine's
moment of discovery, when the penny drops, the illusions of
romance are dispelled, and her real knowledge of life and
society (and therefore of herself) begins. Catherine certainly
thinks so; and, having been bolstered by Henry's good sense,
she banishes from her mind any dark suspicions that pop into

41

it, as Eleanor shifts nervously outside the bedroom door with news of Catherine's calamitous reversal of fortune, her sudden banishment from Northanger Abbey. Far from equipping Catherine with the good sense to see her social world for what it really is, Henry has merely supplanted one kind of illusion (constructed out of the florid fantasies of Gothic romance) with another (the civil complacencies of Home Counties England). Disarmed by Henry, Catherine is completely unprepared for the General's Gothic offensiveness. Austen's ironic vision is such that no statement, no matter how unexceptionable, is left unqualified for long. Equally, none of her characters ever speaks directly for Austen, for what Austen has to say involves, not momentary certitudes, but an ever-vigilant process of introspection and self-knowledge. Thus Henry, as well as Catherine, must learn, as he implicitly does in the course of limiting the damage his father caused in the wake of Henry's misleading speech. Nor is learning a matter of simply internalizing someone else's views, which is what Catherine does with Henry's lecture. She has merely exchanged one faulty authority for another, where authority is faulty because it is not derived from one's own hard-won experience. Catherine's true moment of recognition is thus not her internalization of Henry's homily, but the moment, after her reconciliation with the Tilneys, where she reflects, in her own language rather than Henry's, on the General being, if not quite a wife abuser in the manner of Radcliffe's Marquis Mazzini (from *A Sicilian Romance*), still a not very 'nice' man.

To put matters another way, Austen is as inventive in ringing the changes on discovery and reversal as she is on comic obstacles. In *Emma*, the heroine goes through a whole series of 'recognitions', each one, she confidently believes, the last, until her incorrigible belief in her own judgement leads her into yet another humiliating acknowledgement that her previous discovery was premature. This false series of recognitions comes to a head, when, finally humbled, with great stoicism she accepts that her suspicions regarding Harriet's and Mr Knightley's marital intentions really are true, and, armed with this false knowledge, immediately finds herself at cross purposes with Mr Knightley's proposal of marriage. Thus, even in the moment of greatest interest to herself, when she thinks she finally sees, Emma is blind. Thematically, this is part of the novel's exploration of the view that the communal wisdom ought to prevail over the upstart individual, who, presuming to know more and better than her peers, sets about arranging and meddling in the affairs of others, where romantic affairs are a synecdoche for social matters. Reversal only comes about for Emma, she is only finally guided to her proper place in the social order, when she accepts, finally, the provisionality of things, the otherness of others that must finally render their affairs opaque to lookers-on.

In *Pride and Prejudice* reversal attends upon the recognition of the two principals that they were, in their separate ways, wrong; but it is part of the vision of the novel that acceptance of such revisions of oneself – revisions mediated through one's knowledge of oneself as a social being, necessarily involving ideologies of rank and station, of 'class' – is extremely difficult. Hence the resolution waits upon the accidents of time and place, as the lovers negotiate their way towards each other through the maze of social complications. *Persuasion* has a similar structure, with the difference that the moment of recognition of past error precedes the action. The discovery that comes upon Anne Elliot at the close of the story is not something about herself, but something about Captain Wentworth: that he loves her still. This has been clear to the reader for some time; and the reader's awareness of the precarious nature of the lovers' happiness, that so much depends upon the chance to let their feelings be known to one another, brings home to the reader the potentially tragic power of social convention, which through its very abstract concreteness can become a real barrier to human happiness. In *Mansfield Park* a collective recognition follows hard on the heels of the calamitous reversals inflicted by the Crawfords. The device of recognition and reversal is thus of a piece with the process of education that structures this, like all other Austen novels.

THE NOVEL OF MANNERS

So far, then, I have identified two different generic aspects of the Austenian novel: Austen's resourceful use of comic structures and her development of the novel of education. The two aspects reflect each other, as the heroine resolves the comic obstacles through self-knowledge, through learning about herself, her world, and what she owes to each. Another way of putting it would be to say that Austen has novelized the comedy of manners. If we take Frances Burney's *A Busy Day* as a model, the influence becomes readily apparent. The comedy of manners, which includes, for instance, Sheridan's *The School for Scandal* and *The Rivals*, looks back to the Jacobean City comedy, and features clearly recognizable social types placed in a situation where they are bound to misunderstand each other, as country gentlemen, men of the world, 'cits' (men of trade from the City of London), and various aristocratic and sub-aristocratic types promiscuously mix in the pursuit of cash or women or men or status or a mixture of all four. Austen did not know Burney's play. It was never performed and was first published in the twentieth century. Nevertheless *A Busy Day* resembles *Sense and Sensibility* in several ways, a resemblance pointing to a common, generic matrix.

At this point it is worth noting a peculiar nuance of the English word 'city', which I will come back to later. At this time Britain could boast of several cities, such as, for instance, Edinburgh, or, in England, Bristol and Norwich. 'City', nevertheless, signified London; and not just London, but its financial centre. 'City' may therefore signify, not just the metropolis, but the financial centre that was already well entrenched as the capital engine of imperial expansion. A 'cit' might signify a tradesman, but it could equally imply someone involved in the City trade, meaning powerful financial instruments, with lucrative rewards. The City was by no means the preserve of an upwardly mobile bourgeoisie; it was also characterized by purveyors of what the economic historians P. J. Cain and A. G. Hopkins refer to as 'gentlemanly capitalism', meaning members of landed wealth, also active in the City.[21] Hence the rich nuance of the term 'city': it could mean the town, as opposed to the country; or, negatively, London as the 'Great Wen', the blemish on the face of an otherwise rural England. It was the place of 'trade'; but it was also the locus of the wealth that was transforming England, where middling members of society promiscuously mixed with the great lords, and where social boundaries dissolved through that powerful solvent, money, or, as it becomes when there is enough of it, 'capital' (another word that catches the peculiarly English association of its major city with finance in transforming abundance). Burney's play brings these connotations of the 'city' to the fore. It concerns the courtship and marriage of Eliza Watts, an heir to a large city fortune, and an upper-class young man named Cleveland. The play begins with the couple's fresh arrival from India. Cleveland believes he has been summoned by his uncle, Sir Marmaduke Tylney, to receive his inheritance; in fact, his uncle wishes him to marry an heiress named Miss Percival in order to pay off his mortgage. In the meantime Eliza lodges with her guardians, a family of wealthy, vulgar, city traders. Cleveland is doubly embarrassed: by his uncle's plan, and by the low connections of his fiancée, whose existence he keeps secret, fearing the snobbish displeasure of his family. As with the Ferrar brothers in *Sense and Sensibility*, the hero has a foppish sibling, Frank, who is very much à la mode. Complications begin when Frank himself begins to court Eliza in order to pay off his debts. Miss Percival discovers Cleveland's secret engagement and leagues together with Frank by arranging a meeting between Eliza's *parvenu* relatives and Sir Marmaduke's family in the mistaken belief that snobbery will put an end to Eliza's claims. Instead, the size of Eliza's fortune dissipates the family prejudice and resolves the complications. In the meantime, the wide mix of social types leads to a great deal of mutual quizzing of manners across the divides of 'rank'.

In novelizing the comedy of manners Austen makes three significant innovations. Rather than simply mimicking the drama's detached observation of the action, as if it were happening on stage before us, she locates the reader close to her heroine through free indirect speech, thus providing a partial point of view; she unites the untying of complications with a learning process on the part of the heroine, a process the reader vicariously shares, or undergoes, as a result of Austen's management of point of view; and, finally, she seizes on the fundamental point that it is through manners that we know others, as well as ourselves. The artistic acceptance of the final point has several further consequences. First, it restrains the impulse towards satire, as knowledge of the other, rather than pleasure in the other's foibles, takes precedence (it is part of Austen's artistic manners that it is bad manners to 'quiz' for it own sake, a hostility possibly registered in her reference to, in a letter to Cassandra, 'a monstrous deal of stupid quizzing'[22]); and it imparts an air of realism to the work. In transforming the genre into prose fiction, Austen tones down and complicates the comedy of manners, although figures typical of the drama's broad comedy are vestigially present, such as the cit's daughter (Mrs Elton); the cit's widow (Mrs Jennings); the city fop (Robert Ferrars); the snob (Lady Catherine de Bourgh; Sir Walter Elliott); or the self-made man (Captain Wentworth).

Austen's realism, then, is partly a function of her refusal of the overdrawn. Her flair for the grotesque, for caricature, is carefully reined in; and, when it is given its head, it is often in preparation for an ambuscade of the unwary reader, of which the most celebrated instance is the Box Hill episode from *Emma*. Under duress from the challenge posed to her social supremacy by the obnoxious Mrs Elton, and determined to dominate the dull party through high-spirited banter with Frank Churchill, Emma unpardonably lets herself go, utterly deflating the tedious Miss Bates with a single devastating act of repartee. Miss Bates is herself a stock character, one drawn on the model of Shakespeare's tiresome, prolix low-lifes, characters too witless ever to arrive at a point. As far as this stock character goes, Miss Bates is a fine example, but even so the reader is surely as wearied by her directionless inanities as Emma is, and doubtless glories, vicariously, in the crushing of her. Frank Churchill calls upon the party to say one clever thing, or two things moderately so, or 'three things very dull indeed' (*E*. 306). With ready self-deprecation (a self-assessment mixed in with her knowledge of her social dependency), Miss Bates blurts out that she shall say 'three dull things as soon as ever I open my mouth' (*E*. 306). Emma's deadly riposte – politely couched and so much the worse for being so – is that Miss Bates will have trouble confining herself to 'only three at once' (*E*. 306). And just as Emma is taken to task by Mr Knightley for her bad manners – bad manners that threaten the stability of the community, which must encompass high and low, the acute and the obtuse – so, too, is the reader exposed in her illicit moment of *schadenfreude*. Mr Knightley pointedly asks how Emma could 'be so insolent' in her wit 'to a woman of her character, age, and situation?' (*E.* 309), a question to which Emma has only humiliating answers. It is an important moment in Emma's moral education, where she learns to see beyond the caricatured surface of a personality taken at face value, and in isolation from larger concerns. It is a matter of twofold depth: the depth of the character herself, of Miss Bates having other sides (such as a good heart); and the depth of the social field in which the perception takes place – what one might call the social and moral context of knowing others, a form of knowing bound up with the novel's exploration of community. In other words, in an Austen novel, not only is character three dimensional, but so is the social setting in which character is known. If coming to know this is part of the heroine's education, it is an education shared by the reader. Both aspects are in play, for instance, in Elinor Dashwood's overcoming of her fastidious first impressions of Mrs Jennings's vulgarity.

If a sense of the complication of character contributes to Austen's realism, so too does her steady focus on manners as the medium of social knowledge. Linguistically, manners are metonyms, where individual words come to stand for, or at any rate implicate, the class of things to which they belong. Thus, to take a modern instance, if one were to say of a character that he wore 'green wellies', the reader might infer that he also drove a Range Rover, had a Barbour jacket, worked in the City with a place in the country, and had a relish for claret. If it turned out that the character with green wellies lived on a council estate, say, as an owner-occupier, this piece of information might be interpreted very differently: one might surmise the character had unrealistic social ambitions, or conversely, none at all, and was unaware of the social incongruity in his attire. Novelists draw upon the metonymic power of 'manners' to create expectations in the reader, which they satisfy, or complicate, as the case may be. The point that concerns us here is that a novelist who proceeds to create character through the medium of manners – through metonymic associations – will be imparting to his or her work a sense of realism, of social observation. The sense a novel may succeed in giving us, of observing a vanished world, with its delicate intangibilities in a ghostly fashion somehow present, is principally derived from the associative force of manners. If John Thorpe stands before us, in the mind's eye, as a rematerialized Georgian 'rattle', with his fashionable slang and barouche, it is because Austen has captured his 'manners'. It is a force Austen realized in her novels perhaps better than any of her fictional antecedents.[23]

By way of contrast, consider the Gothic novel. It, too, is highly metonymic, as all language is; but it uses metonyms differently. Matthew Lewis's Madrid, or Ann Radcliffe's Naples, are not accurate representations of these places; the metonymic associations of the manners they observe are circulated via travel books, other novels, religious pamphlets, English cultural preconceptions, or the conventions of romance. No one would read *The Monk* and wonder over a vanished way of life. In the Gothic, metaphors, rather than metonyms, predominate, at least as far as the immediate impact of the narrative is concerned. Thus the haunted house, or castle, which all true specimens of the genre possess, from *The Castle of Otranto* to the *Blair Witch Project*, shimmers as an overdetermined image of the body, with its hidden, uncontrollable forces, its recesses and depths; as a dysfunctional symbol of the home; or as the embodiment of a destructive, inalienable past. When Henry Tilney teases Catherine Morland about her Gothic expectations, it is precisely the symbolic possibilities of the Gothic castle, a ruin chock-a-block with mysteries, that Henry fixes upon, and that Catherine projects onto the bland surface of a modernized Northanger Abbey. As a novelist, rather than a romancer, Austen is making the sly point that Catherine has been doing the wrong kind of reading; it is the novel and not romance – certainly not Gothic romance – that helps us read or penetrate the mystery of other people's manners. If there is, after all, a kind of Gothic reality in what is happening to Catherine, in being abducted to an abbey by a patriarchal tyrant intent on cementing a marriage of alliance, it is something she cannot see, because she has read too many Gothic romances: she insists on reading metaphorically, rather

48

than metonymically. It is only when Catherine learns to be a nice judge of manners that she is able to know the General for what he really is: a not very nice, somewhat tyrannical, old-fashioned member of the gentry with stiff, avaricious notions.

PASTORALS

As we have seen, the air of realism Austen's novels generate is owing to a concatenation of fictional effects. Her characters undergo a process of social education within the boundaries of the probable. Instead of disclosing outlandish mysteries, her characters learn whom it is they really love, whom they have been unfair to, whom they have prejudged, or whom they have not judged severely enough. Eventually first-hand knowledge comes to them of where their responsibilities lie, to both themselves and to others. It is a process of education – an inevitable movement towards resolution and marriage – undercut and rendered 'natural' by false recognitions and premature disentanglements that serve to impart a sense of complexity to the inevitable arc of the comic plot. At the same time, this process of social and subjective knowing is mediated through manners, which imparts a sense of the real to the work. And finally, through references to improbable genres, such as the Gothic, Austen succeeds in imparting a sense, not so much of the probable, as of the complicated real.

This is, of course, an illusion. Realism is a comparative term; we may say that one work conforms to our expectations of the real more than another; or we may say that our generic expectations of the real have a history, in which some works are more significant than others in the fictional construction of 'realism'. Even apart from these critical bromides, Austen's 'realism' is an illusion; for, as much as her novels are realistic essays in social education, they are also comic pastorals. All of her major novels are, in one way or another, pastorals. In all of them there is a tension, or movement, between country and city. Her narratives begin in the country, in some premonition of rural bliss; they then move to the city, or have the city move to them, an action that brings the complications (not necessarily the obstacles) the love plot will resolve; and end with a pastoral closure back in the country. Like all Austen's acts of fictional artifice, it is done with a finesse that hides its own conceit. Nevertheless, the pastoral is a crucial instrument in Austen's art of realism.[24]

The pastoral structure I have described is the least evident in *Emma*, Austen's most pastoral work. The paradox is easily explained: it is because *Emma* is so devoted to the pastoral ideal that the threat from the city (in the double sense I earlier referred to) is at its most attenuated. It is, nevertheless, residually present. Mr Knightley may be destined to a harmonious country life, as the elder brother, but John Knightley's lot is a deracinating sojourn in the city, where he labours as a lawyer, a dislocation that may explain the grumpiness he brings with him on his visits from London. Through Emma's meddling, two representatives of city wealth, or trade, are brought into the community, where they threaten havoc: Mrs Elton and Harriet Smith, both tradesmen's daughters, and one of them illegitimate at that. Both of them, in different senses of the phrase, are put in their place; and, indeed, socially speaking, *Emma* is about 'place'. However, *Emma* is unusual in associating vulgarity (usually meaning, for Austen, wrong notions about place) almost solely with her city representatives, although matters might have been different if we had seen more of Mrs Churchill. Usually, members of the upper gentry and aristocracy are principal members of Austen's crew of vulgarians. *Emma*'s difference in this respect is another mark of that novel's working with (although she never fully works with) the conservative grain of the pastoral.

Life in a country parsonage is at the heart of Austen's treatment of pastoral: a parsonage, not because Austen's vision is a religious one, although there are overtones of it, but because it represents an appropriate, pastoral *via media*. A parsonage, with a good living, is not so dangerous as a great house with its social webs linking it to London and Bath, nor does it represent the kind of indigence that might sorely try one's powers of civility. Socially, it is ideally situated between the needy poor and the heedless rich. Environmentally, a parsonage garden is the aesthetic realization of ecological self-sufficiency, equally distant from growing food for money and the otiose grounds of large country mansions, with their capacities to transform the landscape merely for the purposes of show and consumption (something that Austen's landowner heroes, such as Mr Knightley and Darcy, resist). According to country, Tory ideology, the parsonage stood at the centre of community, with its beautifully modulated gradations of rank, station, obligations, duties, and rights. The great, landed house may have been at the apex of this vision of community, but it was the parsonage that really embodied its ideals. Remote from distorting ambitions – from the temptation of grand alliances with the great, political families, or from the bait of the wealthy tradesman's daughter – the parsonage looked to the community for its life, entertainment, and meaning.

The parsonage is not just central to Austen's heroines' expectations; it is often the fulcrum of their understanding. Catherine Morland learns to prefer the country virtues of the Woodston parsonage to the factitious glamour of abbeys. Elinor Dashwood's ideal, from first to last, is a cosily situated parsonage; the fact that the one her virtue deserves is attached to a country house in which her beloved sister presides is mere icing on the cake. Not only has Fanny Price no ambition for anything other than life in a parsonage with Edmund; through the rectitude of her own moral vision she helps Edmund realize its ideological meaning, its organic purpose, nudging him back onto his true course as a second son with a redeeming desire for meaningful work (a situation much like Edward Ferrars in *Sense and Sensibility*).

Austen's novels are not just pastorals in the sense of being works set in an idealized place halfway between the corrupt city and savage nature; they are self-conscious pastorals; pastorals as political vision. Austen's world was a highly politicized one, marked by huge city gatherings of working-men, inspired by *The Rights of Man*; by radicals arguing for the renovation of the ancient constitution; by revolutionary slaughter in France and treason trials at home.[25] It was impossible not to be political, for indifference to politics was itself politically understood. In this context, Austen's pastorals are nicely poised. The world of her fictions is not one where hierarchy is automatically endorsed, and obviously, still less, is it one where the social order is systematically undermined. Rather,

51

her social world is one of permeable boundaries and social flux, where aristocratic bullies are brought to heel, and where room is made for meritorious tradesmen. Equally, it is a world where the social order reasserts itself, with the vulgarians cast out, whether nouveau riche or old money. To put it another way, Austen's texts do not unthinkingly endorse a conservative ideology; rather they explore what such an ideology might mean, in concrete social terms. Her pastorals are not simple exercises in nostalgia, but complex representations of a social order, an 'organic' community, capable of growing, regulating, and healing itself, by containing or expelling the bad and internalizing the good (essentially the story of *Mansfield Park*). The Revolution debates and the Regency crisis both raised urgent questions on how the country was to be run best. Austen's texts answer that question through her version of a dynamic, which is to say, a responsive, changing, 'pastoral' society.[26] I say 'pastoral', in this particular instance, because 'rural' will not do. Austen's communities are not cut-off country backwaters. On the contrary, they are networked with the centres of imperial power (in the way that, for instance, Henry Crawford can procure an important naval commission for Fanny's brother, direct from the Admiralty in Whitehall). They are linked to the city, without being of it; a connection and distance that is very much part of the political vision of Austen's pastorals, with their representations of how English society might renew itself, thus forestalling dangerous, revolutionary energies.

The education theme is thus not only a part of the comic plot; it is central to Austen's version of pastoral, as it is through education, through the citizens' capacities to learn from, and regulate, each other, that Austen's pastoral societies heal and renew themselves. As mentioned earlier, *Emma* is the most straightforward embodiment of Austen's pastoral vision: indeed, one could call it a Tory pastoral. The novel begins with its own version of the Regency crisis: although Mr Woodhouse is not mad, he is prematurely aged, and as such has lost the capacity to govern the house (or nation), save through a manipulative invalidism.[27] Emma, as the Regent, threatens to run amok, having lost her governess, the sensible Miss Taylor, now Mrs Weston.

A key aspect of Tory ideology was the visibility of landed wealth. Land brought with it rights and duties. It was also spread out before the community, for all to see. It was thus immediately clear whether the custodians of the country fulfilled their obligations as well as their privileges: whether the bond of mutual respect, dependency, and well-being that subsisted between landowner and tenant was maintained, or let go. Mr Knightley is just such an idealized member of the landed wealth. He may enjoy the respect, deference, and a share of the farming profits of Robert Martin, but Robert Martin in turn enjoys the support and attention of Mr Knightley. As a result of this healthy bond, both reap the rewards of an enlightened husbandry. Harriet Smith, on the other hand, is the living synecdoche of the evils of commercial wealth, of capital, which is invisible, and therefore not subject to the correcting scrutiny of its possessor's neighbours. In the enlightened community of Highbury, Harriet Smith is not held accountable for the stigma of her birth. But, as the illegitimate daughter of some wealthy Lord in London, or tradesman who got his money, nobody knows how, or where, or from whom, she is, in her person (and here I refer to the period of the story when her birth is yet a mystery), an all too vivid embodiment of the social irresponsibility of invisible cash. In romanticizing Harriet's origins, Emma not only builds on sand. She commits a significant act of social irresponsibility by promoting the illegitimate claims of invisible wealth, which, like Harriet's own father, takes its pleasure and then washes its hands of the consequences. Marriage to Robert Martin represents the healing powers of the pastoral vision. Mr Knightley has interceded on Martin's behalf, has given him sound advice, while Harriet is to be rewarded for her personal virtues in spite of her background, which is redeemed by the act of marriage. Emma's intercession is thus a disaster, not just for Harriet, but for the governance of the community: it represents a promotion of the baseless over the sound, and the empty glamour wealth surrounds itself with, over a true assessment of the status and interests of the community's members. Politically speaking, Emma's 'Regency', from the time of Miss Taylor's departure, to her marriage to Mr Knightley, is a period of misrule, including interference in Harriet's life, the disastrous alienation of Mr Elton (especially damaging given his position as vicar), her impercipience in the affair between Frank Churchill and Jane Fairfax, and the humiliation of Miss Bates. Emma's dangerous disaffiliation from the tenets of Tory ideology is very lightly revealed to us in the following speech from her, in which she seeks to undermine Harriet's attachment to Robert Martin:

> 'Mr Martin, I imagine, has his fortune entirely to make – cannot be at all beforehand with the world. Whatever money he might come into when his father died, whatever his share of the family property, it is, I dare say, all afloat, all employed in his stock, and so forth; and though, with diligence and good luck, he may be rich in time, it is next to impossible that he should have realised any thing yet.' (E. 27)

The full significance of the passage becomes apparent only when we understand the contemporary ambiguity of the word 'realize'. Its primary meaning (beyond 'to make real') was 'to convert securities into cash', or 'property into money' (OED). In the context of insecure speculations, such as the South Sea Bubble, to realize wealth was to convert paper profits into ready money. Dr Johnson provides a secondary meaning, which inverts the first: for Johnson, 'to realize' is 'to convert money into land'. Through the interstices of Emma's perspective we are able to see that Robert Martin is associated with the Johnsonian meaning of converting wealth into land, whereas Emma employs the term's first meaning. She imagines, or speculates, on how Robert Martin, with 'diligence and good luck', may transform his floating 'stock' (the pun is calculated) into yet more wealth. For Emma, 'realize' means to profit through stock. Whereas Robert Martin is grounded in the land, Emma talks like a stockjobber, an insight that reverses the thrust of her speech, for it is herself, rather than Robert Martin, who is revealed to us as a figure of unrooted wealth.

Mr Knightley might be said eventually to cure Emma of her speculative fever. As a character he is pivotal to the novel's pastoral vision. He is also the antidote to Emma's speculation. He is the incarnation of the socially responsible landowner, leading by example, dispensing sound advice and knitting together the community. He is also an important counterweight to the commercial evils of the city. His fraternal bond with John Knightley keeps the uncertain temper of the latter in check on his return from his toil as a lawyer in London; his good offices ensure the integration of the Coles into Highbury's first society; and he is an obvious foil to Mrs Elton's vulgarity. Mrs Elton's dangerous status is emphasized by her Bristol origins, a city famous for deriving its wealth from slaving, the epitome of a dirty industry. While there is no indication that Mrs Elton's own wealth derives from the slave trade, a connection is drawn between her ostentatious manners, with her conspicuous carriage rides (in contrast to Mr Knightley's pedestrian habits), and rootless money. To use the language we must presume to be Emma's, Mrs Elton, a merchant's daughter, 'brought no name, no blood, no alliance' (*E*. 152). In a sense, Mrs Elton's presence in Highbury is Emma's doing, as it was owing to her blundering that Elton married quickly, on the rebound. It is not the case that *Emma* is against new money: it is rather that it envisages social progress as a matter of absorbing new money into the community, in the manner of the Coles, where they imbibe socially responsible values, rather than remaining outside, as a vulgar menace. In one sense you could say that the Coles are made to know, and acknowledge, their place in the hierarchy; but by the same token Emma is brought to recognize it as well, an action that is very much to the advantage of the Coles. The problem with Mrs Elton is that she is beyond knowing, despite her famous 'resources'.

Mr Knightley is pivotal to the novel's pastoral vision, partly through his personal qualities, but equally through his position as heir to Donwell Abbey. As we shall see in the chapter on free indirect speech, more than any other of Austen's novels, *Emma* is locked into the perceptions of its main character. As a result the novel is reticent about one of its leading ironies, which is that Emma does not have the right she implicitly assumes in governing the romantic lives of the community; the right that comes with being a member of its first family. It is a 'right' she abuses, and grows out of; but even the premise is false, for the first house is Donwell Abbey, and not Hartfield. Donwell Abbey is the landed estate: Hartfield's wealth is comparatively mysterious. Presumably Mr Woodhouse is a member of the 'three per cents', someone living off cash invested in the city.[28] As such, ideologically, Emma's position is much closer to the Eltons and the Coles, whom she affects to patronize. Austen sows clues undermining Emma's snobbish illusions throughout her narrative. For instance, Robert Martin calls upon John Knightley at Brunswick Square, in London. A contemporary reviewer alerts us to the significance of this: 'when we are occasionally transported to London, our authoress has the originality to waive Grosvenor or Berkeley-squares, and sets us down in humble Brunswick-square.'[29] The modesty of John Knightley's London residence deflates Emma's pretensions. Humble Brunswick Square, moreover, is represented to us as a liminal space, where a variety of ranks mix together: as such it is a sign of capital growth and the social flux such growth creates. Accordingly, it is entirely appropriate that Robert Martin and John Knightley, the tenant farmer and lawyer, should dine there together. Such social mixing, happening quietly in the background, undermines Emma's snobbishness, her fruitless attempts at maintaining pointless social divisions. The narrative takes Emma from a false premise to a more enlightened understanding: society and rank are not fixed but mutable.

The point becomes clearer when we consider one of *Emma's* central tropes: circulation. Throughout the eighteenth century, social commentators had expressed great anxiety over the consequences of Britain's growing economy: the growth of luxury and the proliferation of consumer goods. As a result, there was a great increase in unregulated circulation (unregulated, that is, save by the market place's 'invisible hand'): of goods, news, books, information, and, with these, peoples and classes. Austen, in *Emma*, does not, King Canute like, simply resist this tide of circulation: she imagines rather a contest between good and bad forms of it. If the Eltons, and their ostentatious carriage, are the epitome of bad circulation, Mr Knightley represents the good: he is forever on the move, nurturing Highbury, ensuring that circulation is merely a means of quickening the community's lifeblood. Emma's initial position, as an unselfconscious daughter of a '3 per cent', selfishly meddling in the affairs of others, is the embodiment of blocked, unhealthy, circulation (so that we can say that the father's invalidism is ideologically recapitulated in the daughter). It is only when she marries Mr Knightley, and becomes mistress of Donwell Abbey, that her assumed position, and her real one, coincide; but by then she has learned, or made progress towards learning, the true nature of her responsibilities, as well as her powers.

Emma is at once Austen's most pastoral work, and her most conservative: conservative, at least, as far as endorsing the social order is concerned, however qualified (remembering as well that it is in her qualifications that Austen's critics find purchase for their counter-conservative readings). Moreover, to judge Austen's political position on the basis of one novel would be an act of great critical incaution, as her novels sketch out a variety of positions, some complementary, others verging on contradiction. This becomes readily apparent if we compare *Emma* with *Persuasion*, Austen's least pastoral work. If in *Emma* the landed gentry are the pillar of the community, in *Persuasion* the pillar has collapsed. The class that is so ideally represented in *Emma* by Mr Knightley is pilloried in *Persuasion* in the lamentable form of Sir Walter Elliot, a vain, autocratic, selfish, incompetent boob of a baronet, who has left his estate mismanaged and encumbered, and who aspires to surround himself in Bath, where he has been forced to retire through his own profligacy, by other, equally worthless members of Debrett's *Baronetage*. As a class, the landed gentry come off a distinct second best to the seafaring self-made men, Admiral Croft and Captain Wentworth. Lady Russell is the only possible, positive representative of the class Mr Knightley so ably represented in *Emma*. Even then, although gentry, and 'exceedingly well provided for', Lady Russell is not landed. Moreover, she is put in the decidedly equivocal position of having offered the heroine the strictly correct but effectively wrong advice of abiding by her family's prejudices and refusing Wentworth, advice Anne Elliott spends seven years emotionally, if not intellectually, repenting.

If *Persuasion* is Austen's least pastoral work, it is possibly because it is the one most touched by history, by acknowledgement of the profound changes sweeping through Georgian society. Uppercross cottage, inhabited by Mary and Charles Musgrove, is the kind of house that in a different work

Austen might well have presented as a pastoral *via media* – not too large, nor too poor – but instead she renders it in a spirit of domestic realism. Not only does Austen refrain from endorsing any hints of a placidly happy family life; she particularizes the domestic space in terms of new architectural and domestic fashions: we hear of French Doors, sofas, and carpets. Uppercross cottage is presented in pointed contrast to the old-fashioned austerities of Kellynch Hall, which has none of these modish comforts.[30] More to the point, the Musgrove home signifies the deep penetration of commerce, fashion, and consumption. Austen had represented the world of contemporary luxury before, but, as in *Northanger Abbey*, she had tended to restrict the signs of commerce (and therefore luxury) to towns, such as Bath, or to the great houses closely linked with the city. Reaching deep into the country, the power of commerce – much the same thing as the power of history – disrupts the equilibrium of Austen's pastoral vision. Alternatively, one might say that her waning faith in the indigenous community's ability to reform itself led the way to a more critical view. However one regards it, *Persuasion* appears at once a more nostalgic text, gripped by a sense of the pastness of the past, and one alive to the inevitabilities of historical change. Thus the departure of the Elliots from Kellynch Hall, and the arrival of the Crofts, although presented as a renewal, is yet suffused with a sense of a changing order. Croft's new wealth, like Wentworth's, is a sign of the times, representing, as it does, the profits to be had from the contintental war, for able captains willing to risk danger in order to profiteer off enemy ships.

I think it significant that *Persuasion* is alone of Austen's novels in not envisaging very clearly the place – the new home – in which the heroine is to spend her life. As we have seen, in Austen's pastorals, the domus, the topography of the house, is metonymically alive with suggestions of a larger social vision. We know, of course, that Captain Wentworth will eventually buy some place in the country, quite likely near the Crofts now residing in Anne's old home, where the couple will settle down as the Captain's seafaring days draw to a close. But the very lack of specificity is suggestive of a larger uncertainty about the material shape of the community. It is not as if Anne

Elliot were indifferent to the idea of a home. On the contrary, her desire for a home is every bit as strong as – is indeed entangled with – her desire for a husband. She is ' "nobody" at Kellynch, only a guest at Lady Russell's, a glorified au pair at Uppercross, and then an additional person in the rented rooms at Bath less prized even than Mrs Clay'.[31] Chapter XVII begins with Anne Elliot visiting her old schoolfriend, Mrs Smith, now a poor invalid resident in the unfashionable Westgate Buildings in Bath. How déclassé an address can be gauged by Sir Walter Elliot's horrified reaction at the mere thought of a daughter of his paying the place a visit, even if it is only Anne. The Westgate Buildings were in fact scouted as a possible address for the Austens when they left Jane's beloved childhood home of Steventon Rectory for Bath, which she never much liked.[32] The chapter appears to reverse this trajectory, as Anne moves from visiting the confined rooms of her impecunious, widowed friend, in Bath, to the possession of her childhood home, at least in her mind. Lady Russell reminds Anne that she shall take possession of Kellynch, if she accepts Walter William Elliot:

> For a few moments her imagination and her heart were bewitched. The idea of becoming what her mother had been; of having the precious name of 'Lady Elliot' first revived in herself; of being restored to Kellynch, calling it her home again, her home forever, was a charm which she could not immediately resist . . . The same image of Mr Elliot speaking for himself brought Anne to composure again. The charm . . . faded away. (P. 143)

Anne is unable to sustain the wish fulfilment. The ideal of the home, and the material house, have become detached. Thus Mrs Croft is able to make a home on a man of war, while Captain Harville transforms his poky rented quarters at Lyme into a 'picture of repose and domestic happiness' (P. 89) through 'ingenious contrivances and nice arrangements' (P. 88). In Austen's earlier novels the ideal home was rooted in a house embedded within the community; in her final novel, the ideal has become mobile, as if in anticipation of rootless modernity.

In her pastoral vision Austen is never doctrinaire. The particular vision of each novel is always in response to the pressure brought to weigh upon the question posed by salient historical events of the period, of how one ought best to shape the community. Austen works with a more or less constant set of variables: a notion of social order or hierarchy; landed wealth; new money; commerce; personal merit; a sense of the pressures imposed by history; leisure, vocation, and marriage. But these variables prove to be highly protean, for, in each of Austen's pastorals, the accents produce very different meanings.

3

Point of View

In a modern novel we take it for granted that dialogue is driven by the subtext, by the unspoken tensions that exist between characters who do not exchange information so much as they obliquely reveal their conscious or unconscious motives. Although such dialogue may strike us as 'natural', it was invented, and in this invention Austen played a significant role. Austen's formal creativity has come increasingly to interest her critics. For instance, Chris Jones argues that unspoken projections shape Austen's dialogue. Her characters project onto others feelings they themselves have problems with, and then respond to these others as if they had expressed these difficult emotions. In one of her most quoted letters, Austen tells her sister Cassandra that she does not write for readers too dull to follow dialogue without abundant help.[1] But, as Jones argues, it is not simply that the reader has to follow who is speaking; she has to reconstruct, and unravel, the unspoken projections and identifications that structure the dialogue.[2] Elsewhere Kathryn Sutherland has argued that Austen was as stylistically innovative in her deployment of speech as Emily Dickinson was in her use of punctuation. Just as Dickinson dispensed with traditional grammatical pointing in order to capture the rhythms and disjunctions of a poetic line unfurling over tonal ironies, so Austen experimented with dialogue: 'In the later, mature novels, Austen became more and more interested in experimenting with conversation, with voices that interrupt each other. A great deal of this relies on a kind of ungrammaticality, on vocal encroachment, and capturing the rhythms of conversation, which are counter-syntactic.'[3] Most current Austen texts are based on R. W.

61

Chapman's 1923 edition, which regularized Austen's punctuation. The new Cambridge edition, currently in preparation, of which Kathryn Sutherland is one of the editors, aims to restore Austen's punctuation to its 'pre-Chapman' state, thus making it easier for the reader to appreciate the nature of Austen's technical innovation.

We have already investigated some aspects of Austen's powerfully deceptive mimetic art: we have glanced at the ways she sustains the illusion of personality and at the way she employs manners as if they were (as indeed they are) a semiotic system, out of which Austen builds something akin to Clifford Geertz's 'thick description'. In this chapter I want to tease out another source of artful illusion, one on which the others, to an extent, depend: her management of point of view. As Sir Walter Scott takes care to make clear in his pioneering review, Austen was not the sole, spontaneous source for the new school of fiction she came to dominate. As Marilyn Butler has established, Jane Austen's art is embedded within the practices of her fellow, but especially sister, novelists, of which the two most significant are Frances Burney and Maria Edgeworth.[4] In her management of point of view, Jane Austen is, technically, brilliantly innovative; but it must also be said that many of these techniques were pioneered by her sister novelists.[5]

Throughout the previous chapters I have had occasion to speak of free indirect speech as the delicate instrument of Austen's management of point of view, on which so much of her art, especially her ambiguity – her twists, turns, and readerly ambushes – depends. Free indirect speech is just one of the techniques Austen employs to take us inside, and outside, the consciousness of her characters. But it is one of her most resourceful and important. One of the advantages of adopting such a narrow focus is that it allows us to see, concretely, how Austen's art changes over her career. She never reuses the same technique, in the same way. Such a project begs the question of what order the novels were written in. While the works of her maturity are unproblematic (that is, there is no reason to doubt the chronology of *Mansfield Park* (1814), *Emma* (1816), and *Persuasion* (1818)), the works of her youth have a far more complicated compositional history. The order of my discussion of *Northanger Abbey* (possibly the first completed, and certainly the last published), *Sense and Sensibility* (1811), and *Pride and Prejudice* (1813), is therefore, to a degree, arbitrary. I expect most readers will be familiar with free indirect speech, but, for the benefit of any who are not, I offer the following, cursory introduction.

Free indirect speech is a fairly simple technique. One can easily bring it to mind by breaking down the description. Direct speech is the speech of a character noted through quotation marks. Indirect speech is merely reported speech, without quotation marks, as in: Nicola said she would go to the store to purchase the croissants. Free indirect speech is exactly that: the free representation of a character's speech, by which one means, not words actually spoken by a character, but the words that typify the character's thoughts, or the way the character would think or speak, if she thought or spoke. Take the instance of the narrator saying: Nicola went to the store to purchase the croissants. This might not appear to be free indirect speech, and, indeed, it might not be. But imagine that Nicola is an informal sort of person, in the midst of more formal people. The narrator might then say: Nicky drove to the shop to get some French buns. In so far as this locution typifies the way Nicky thinks and sees herself in contradistinction to others (as someone who 'drives' and 'gets', and avoids foreign words), it tells us quite a bit about her. In this respect, free indirect speech is a technique cognate with the notation of manners: it gives us words that are metonymically, or socially, significant, as regards the character's origin and outlook. But free indirect speech becomes more complex when it is couched in such a way that we are left wondering whether we are reading the character's thoughts and views about events or other characters, or whether they possess authorial objectivity. That is to say, free indirect speech always introduces an element of irony and hence ambiguity. At a stroke, greater demands are made upon the reader, who must strive to deduce the status of the views she is being presented with. Are these the unreliable, or, at any rate, the qualifiable thoughts of the character, or is it information reliably furnished by the narrator? Through free indirect speech, the reader is drawn into a more dynamic narrative enterprise than in narratives in which the device is absent.[6]

NORTHANGER ABBEY

If *Northanger Abbey* was not the first of Austen's completed novels to be drafted, it was probably the first to be finished. It was sold to a publisher in 1803 (who mysteriously refused to publish it), while internal evidence suggests it was written by 1800.[7] One might argue that it was a novel in which Austen was learning her craft, and that this explains why her use of free indirect speech differs so markedly from her later novels. For instance, consider this example from volume II, chapter VI, where Catherine famously discovers the laundry list, believing it to be, in the manner of Radcliffe's *Romance of the Forest*, a document of great and grisly importance:

> The place in the middle alone remained now unexplored; and though she had 'never from the first had the smallest idea of finding any thing in any part of the cabinet, and was not the least disappointed at her ill success thus far, it would be foolish not to examine it thoroughly while she was about it'. It was some time however before she could unfasten the door ... her quick eyes directly fell on a roll of paper ... her feelings at that moment were indescribable. Her heart fluttered, her knees trembled, and her cheeks grew pale. (*NA*148)

The quotation marks inform us that these are the thoughts of Catherine's inner voice; apart from anything else, we know this because Austen introduces the device at the beginning of the chapter, prefacing a similarly marked speech by telling us that 'these thoughts crossed her' mind (*NA* 143). The quotation marks are, in fact, redundant. The marks tell us that these are the words Catherine addresses to herself, to her inner monitor; but the reader is free to infer this regardless of whether it is marked or not, just as she is free to infer that the language following the closed quotation mark is also Catherine's. It is certainly the language of Minerva Press Gothic, which Catherine has been reading too much of. Thus the description may be a true depiction of Catherine's physical state (fluttering and trembling); or it may be Catherine's self-characterization (seeing her self in her mind's eye) in which there is a degree of self-dramatization.

Austen rarely repeats this device: hereafter, such direct speech, where it is the inner thought of her character, is rendered freely, which is to say, without obtrusive, and unnecessary, quotation marks.[8] One might conclude that it is a technical clumsiness of her artistic immaturity, something she might well have corrected, had she the opportunity.[9] There is no way of knowing. One reason a conclusion might be precipitate is that *Northanger Abbey* is *sui generis*. As part burlesque, it is far less concerned with the complex, moral development of her heroine. Satire requires different things from the management of point of view than psychological complexity does. One might say Austen's use of reported thought is clumsy; or one could say it is simply satirically broad.

Although *Northanger Abbey* differs from Austen's later work in its use of free indirect speech, it is actually a useful point of departure for analysing her employment of the device throughout her career, precisely because it is different: it provides a clear register of change. Some of Austen's critics have been perturbed by *Northanger Abbey*'s mixture of novel and burlesque, naturalism and satire.[10] Perturbed, because the work yokes disparate things together: the broad satire of volume I, based in Bath; and a shift towards a standard novel of manners in volume II, where in the environs of Northanger Abbey Catherine undergoes a psychologically deepening experience. Marilyn Butler argues, to the contrary, that the work coheres around the relationship between fact and fiction, the world and the book. Novels are genres, a form of narrative game, a contract between writers and readers. Game theory encompasses not just genres but social interactions, rituals of engagement with their unspoken rules of the permissible and the forbidden. The burlesque concerns the story of two young girls whose minds have been so addled by novel reading that they fail to distinguish the boundaries between life and fiction. One of the characters, Isabella Thorpe, remains in a muddle regarding the differences between them, especially regarding that which is appropriate to each and the degree to which the contractual engagements of the various games are morally binding; while the other does learn the difference. Put in this way, the differences between burlesque (based on grotesques, or characters unable to learn) and the novel (where education is paramount) dissolve, as these differences find themselves encompassed in a larger, comic vision, where it is possible to find a proper balance between the world outside, and inside, fiction, a movement from obtuseness to insight.[11] As a work about life and fiction, *Northanger Abbey* refuses to endorse a simple, binary opposition. The real, and the fictional, are in fact revealed to be inseparable from each other. In developing this complex theme, Austen's use of free indirect speech plays an important role.

Northanger Abbey depicts Catherine's education; but one could also say it represents her socialization. The narrative starts with the reader being given to understand that Catherine does not possess innate sensibility, the inevitable accoutrement of heroines, as we learn from books. The beginning is deceptively complex, for we are being informed of several things at once: that Catherine's character diverges from those found in romances; that the narrator knows that the reader has read many of these romances, and has formed expectations on the basis of them; and, from the narrator's tone, that the narrator knows the reader has learned to distinguish between fact and fiction. The narrator clearly does not seriously expect the reader to be disappointed or confused by Catherine's divergence from the norms of romantic sensibility, as codified in novels. At the same time, however, she leaves it open as a question: what, indeed, is to be expected? In other words, the narrator begs the question of what is natural. We learn, very quickly, that the narrator does not concur with the fashionable notions of what women are by nature, as codified within the cult of sensibility. However, this cultural construction of 'nature' is left hanging within the novel, as an object of satire (principally through Isabella's affectations of sensibility, like many of Isabella's speech acts, a contradiction in terms: one cannot affect sensibility; one either has it, or one has not). But, if sensibility is not natural, what is? Austen leaves this question unanswered, as it is, indeed, unanswerable; but she does provide us with something, in her statements that Catherine liked to run wild, play cricket, and roll down hills, together with other tomboyish proclivities. And, if Austen does not go as far as Locke in considering the mind a *tabula rasa* at birth, she certainly sees young Catherine's as inchoate, undeveloped, and markedly undeformed by affected sensibility or the marked gender roles codified within it. Such views may not make Austen a feminist, but they do provide a bridge between her and writers such as Mary Wollstonecraft who were then in the process of contesting the gender roles implicit within the Rousseauesque cult of sensibility.[12]

Catherine's 'self', or character, then, is as undeveloped as she herself is unsocialized. As an example of what I mean by socialization, take Henry Tilney's analogy of an agreement to dance with the contract of marriage (*NA* 69–71). Like the narrator herself, Henry adopts an ironic, jocular tone, in which levity conceals seriousness. Henry, of course, knows that the rules of the two 'games', marriage and dancing, are different; but he also understands the contracts entered into for moral pennies are as important as those for moral pounds. Catherine quickly learns this lesson, hence her willingness to break lesser rules, such as those governing the decorum of young ladies, to rush headlong after the Tilneys, through the streets of Bath, brushing aside servants, to tell Eleanor and Henry, breathlessly, that she was indeed respecting their appointment. And, because she does respect the rules of this kind of contract, Henry later respects the rules of marital engagement, when he feels that he, or, more particularly, his designing father, has gone too far down the road of contracted marriage (in the messages father and son have been sending at Northanger Abbey) to back out now that his father has turned as aggressively against the marriage as he had been assiduous in courting it. It is a lesson in socialization that Isabella Thorpe never learns; hence her symbolic position at the end, of being unmarried and isolated on the fringes of the society *Northanger Abbey* cares about.

The progress of Catherine's socialization is registered through free indirect speech. Catherine's unreliable mentor, Isabella Thorpe, leads Catherine astray in two fundamental respects. First, she and her brother John infect Catherine with their slangy language in which a moral register is applied to inappropriate objects. Thus, for instance, Isabella refers to a tear in her gown as an 'evil', while John Thorpe says his horse is without 'vice'. Isabella's second bad example is the indiscriminate consumption of novels, of reading novels merely as commodities to be exchanged, whether literally, or as markers of fashionable consumption. This is damaging, not because Isabella fails to discriminate between good and bad novels, but because she reads literally, rather than for the moral or intellectual sense, and as a result allows herself to be caught up in a cultural discourse where fictional representations of subjectivity (such as sentiment and sensibility) are indistinguishable from social affectation, or fashion. Isabella affects to act like a heroine of sensibility, which only leads her into silliness, insincerity, and bad faith. Catherine eventually escapes Isabella's spell, learning to distinguish between the literal and figurative meanings of fictions, but this does not happen until volume II, after she has left Isabella's sphere of influence. However, in volume I, we observe Catherine beginning to free herself from Isabella by emancipating herself from the confusions of Isabella's morally inappropriate language.

The following example of free indirect speech evinces the consequences of Isabella's wayward mentoring. John Thorpe engages Catherine for the first dance of the ball, only to stand her up. Catherine is left publicly exposed at the edge of the dance floor:

> To be disgraced in the eye of the world, to wear the appearance of infamy while her heart is all purity, her actions all innocence, and the misconduct of another the true source of her debasement, is one of those circumstances which peculiarly belong to the heroine's life, and her fortitude under it what particularly dignifies her character. (*NA* 48–9)

This is, of course, symptomatic of Catherine's adolescent naivety; but it is a callowness peculiarly shaped by Isabella. The inappropriate language of morality and catastrophe is at once Catherine's, and, beyond her, Isabella's. Indeed, beyond Isabella, it is the language of romance inappropriately projected onto an everyday humiliation. The passage is free indirect speech. As such it is a teasing representation of the way Catherine thinks about her experience. It is a form of thought where two categories have become confused: the category of moral actions and the category of petty misfortune.

Paradoxically the first stage of Catherine's socialization is her corruption by Isabella's wayward mentoring. Thematically it represents her initiation into the world of fashion, consumption, and luxury – her journey from Fullerton to Bath. It is simultaneously an introduction into history and culture, or, to put it somewhat differently, into the realities of a market economy where even culture is a commodity, including, for instance, the Gothic, at the time the novel's most modish incarnation. The second stage of Catherine's socialization is her learning to discriminate, to use words appropriately, thus undoing Isabella's category confusions. Fittingly, she learns this lesson at Isabella's expense. Isabella has been trying to bully Catherine into joining the planned outing to Blaize Castle, thus breaking her walking engagement with the Tilneys: 'Catherine thought this reproach strange and unkind. Was it the part of a friend thus to expose her feelings to the notice of others? Isabella appeared to her ungenerous and selfish, regardless of every thing but her own gratification. These painful ideas crossed her mind, though she said nothing' (*NA* 88). Unlike the previous example of free indirect speech, Catherine's language is no longer exaggerated, no longer confuses categories. The language of morality and the object to which it is applied have come into alignment. In the first example, Catherine is revealed to us as being without an independent subjectivity, at least to the extent that she borrows her language, and her sense of self, from Isabella. In the second she exerts her independence and thinks for herself. In making her language her own it becomes a serviceable instrument of insight and judgement.

The two examples of free indirect speech exemplify the difference between burlesque and novel. In so far as Catherine has no language of her own, no independent-mindedness, she is a vehicle for satire; but, as she develops independent views, she becomes a personality and so enters the domain of the novel. The first chapter of volume II starts with an extended passage of Catherine's free indirect speech. It is a sign of things to come, as a great deal of the narration of the second volume is inflected by Catherine's increasingly independent point of view, whereas in volume I we rarely encounter perceptions attributable to an independently minded Catherine. Or rather, much of what there is, is Isabella's, who frequently acts as Catherine's invisible ventriloquist. At this point *Northanger Abbey* introduces a subtle inversion, which is integral to its brilliant design.

In volume I, if Isabella is Catherine's unreliable mentor, Henry Tilney is her tutelary spirit who oversees her education, her emancipation from burlesque into personality and the novel. When Catherine and Isabella first meet, they talk excitedly of 'dress, balls, flirtations, and quizzes' (*NA* 30). As Isabella has four years more experience than Catherine, she takes the lead in inducting her friend into these mysteries. Henry's role, on the other hand, is to quiz the quizzers; in a world of debased communication, effective moral action is achieved, not through positive sermons, but through double negatives, or irony. As the master ironist, Henry appears to be the author's double; indeed, the narrator's quizzing of her heroine's confusions between life and fiction (Catherine's discovery of the laundry bill), and Henry's version of the same thing (his pastiche of Radcliffe's Gothic), appear nearly identical. The identification between the narrator and Henry is strengthened by Henry's echoing the narrator's famous defence of the novel, which is also a defence of the novel against romance (in terms reminiscent of Whateley's), of Burney and Edgeworth against the circulating library fare passed on, at second hand, by Isabella. Henry thus appears to be enforcing two important lessons for Catherine: the importance of the difference between fiction and life, which Catherine learns through a proper appreciation of 'games' (which entails a due recognition of the difference between games); and the difference between overdrawn romance and the probable novel, where the probability of the latter touches philosophically upon the rational appreciation of the 'country and the age' in which one lives, with its laws, neighbourhoods of voluntary spies, and roads and newspapers that lay everything open. Catherine lives out this second lesson in her trajectory as a character, where she moves from a character who thinks of herself in romance terms (developing improbable mysteries) to one who thinks in ways appropriate to the novel, with its naturalistic personalities. She also makes this transition because she learns the lesson directly, and painfully, from Henry, when she speculates, via Radcliffe, on the probability of General Tilney being a wife-murderer, and finds herself arraigned by Henry for it.

The novel thus appears to move along on a single, albeit complex, track: in volume I Isabella plays the major role in

Catherine's education, Henry the minor one: in volume II, the roles are reversed. As Henry's influence grows, so Catherine learns to be a person and grows out of burlesque. She comes to understand the difference between romance and novel, or fiction and life. She begins to use language properly, becomes independent-minded, and is fully socialized when a 'revolution in her ideas' brings her full circle (*NA* 184), when she learns to prefer Woodston parsonage to either Northanger Abbey or Bath. Woodston, we are told, is just like Fullerton, only 'better' (*NA* 184): in other words, she ends where she begins, only on a higher plane, in what one might call a romance form of Tory eschatology.

In fact *Northanger Abbey* thinks dialectically. To put it schematically, in volume I, Isabella is the thesis, Henry the antithesis, and the synthesis Catherine's learning to apply Henry's moral language to Isabella's Bath. In volume II, Henry is the thesis. The antithesis is not Isabella, but the world of romance, especially Gothic romance, with which she is associated. Henry's demotion to 'thesis' is the surprising inversion I earlier referred to. We can come at the reasons behind Henry's demotion, and the nature of the synthesis, from a surprising angle: from the novel's treatment of the theme of blushing.

The theme is actually introduced quite late in the novel, appropriately enough, with Catherine's dawning understanding of sexual desire. The 'amazingly agitated' Isabella throws out some broad hints about James: 'Catherine's understanding began to awake: an idea of the truth suddenly darted into her mind; and, with the natural blush of so new an emotion, she cried out, "Good heaven! – my dear Isabella . . . can you really be in love with James?" ' (*NA* 105). 'Natural blush' is a loaded, highly significant phrase, as we can see by turning to Jean-Jacques Rousseau, the cultural architect of Isabella's characterization. As we saw in chapter 2, Rousseau conceived of women as being naturally artificial or coquettish. Rousseau imagines the state of nature as linguistic and masculine: men naturally communicate through language. Women, on the contrary, have no language for their desires, as nature forbids them from making their sexual feelings known through words. However, nature provides women with an alternative, non-verbal, and therefore artificial language: the language of bodily signs, including, above all else, blushing. For Rousseau, a feminine blush is inherently artificial, even though it comes from nature. To put the matter at its simplest, for Rousseau, women are natural coquettes.

Northanger Abbey mounts a playful yet serious critique of Rousseau. One aspect of this critique concerns Isabella's characterization, the fact that she is transparently not a natural coquette: rather, she is a coquette by affectation and culture, a fact counter to Rousseau's point. Through the characterization of Catherine, Austen mounts a yet deeper critique. At one point Austen guys those male authorities who pronounce it improper for women to take the initiative in courtship, by suggesting that young ladies should not dream of gentlemen, unless the gentleman dreams first (*NA* 27). Austen's point is not simply that desire is involuntary: it is that women may express an interest in men outside the medium of coquetry. This is basically the story of Catherine, who is transparent in her desire for Henry without being coquettish and who takes the initiative without the stratagems, affectations, and duplicities fostered by Isabella. Her forwardness is delicately set out through free indirect speech. The following thoughts run through her head, as she hurries after the Tilneys to countermand John Thorpe's cancellation of their date:

> Setting her own inclination apart, to have failed a second time in her engagement to Miss Tilney, to have retracted a promise voluntarily made only five minutes before, and on a false pretence too, must have been wrong. She had not been withstanding them on selfish principles alone, she had not consulted her own gratification; *that* might have been ensured in some degree by the excursion itself, by seeing Blaize Castle ... (*NA* 90–1)

Here Catherine thinks in her new-found language of moral independence; she is also self-deluded, as it is clear to the reader, as it is to the Tilneys, that she is thinking not just of her immediate engagement with Eleanor, but of a future one with Henry. Although she does indeed act in accordance with what she thinks is right, she also consults her own gratification. The fact that this is transparent to others, but not to herself, is one of the characteristics that recommends her to Henry. He is attracted to her, not because she is a coquette, but because she is candid.

'Natural blush' derives its meaning from Austen's argument against the pervasive sexualization of the female body. Within the world of the novel, women, as much as men, make love with their minds. Thus blushing recurs in numerous contexts, only one of them signalling sexual desire, that is, when Catherine recalls an anodyne phrase in James's letter, onto which she has projected her private thoughts, and which she fears Henry will intuit, should he read it (*NA* 178). Otherwise, Catherine blushes at being called good natured (*NA* 118); at Isabella's coquettish behaviour (*NA* 132); at being surprised by Eleanor rummaging in a chest (*NA* 144); and at the 'consummate art of her own question' to Eleanor, designed to elicit, not indications of Henry's reciprocal desire, but intelligence relative to the General's abusive treatment of his wife (*NA* 157). Elsewhere, Isabella runs true to her stereotype, when she blushes at the recollection of her efforts to ensnare Captain Tilney (*NA* 128); but most significantly of all, Henry blushes at having to explain his father's behaviour to Catherine:

> Catherine ... heard enough to feel, that in suspecting General Tilney of either murdering or shutting up his wife, she had scarcely sinned against his character, or magnified his cruelty.
>
> Henry, in having such things to relate of his father, was almost as pitiable as in their first avowal to himself. He blushed for the narrow-minded counsel which he was obliged to expose. (*NA* 215)

This is significant, first, because it breaks down the gender binary implicit in Rousseau's sexual stereotyping (men blush as much as women), thus serving as a metonym for the reality that forever intrudes into such neat oppositions; and, secondly, because it signals that Henry's tutelage has also been, like Isabella's, a partial knowledge from which Catherine must emancipate herself if she is to be a full person. Just as in volume I Catherine had to free herself from Isabella's influence in order to arrive at an objective assessment of her friend, so in volume II she has had to escape from Henry in order to meet him on equal ground. One aspect of her emancipation is a coming to understand that things are more complicated than Henry's neat moralizing allows.

The thematic complexity of the book lies in the way it ties Catherine's intellectual growth to the disruption of the binaries it has previously set up. For example, we earlier saw how the narrator appears to be foursquare behind Henry's quizzical discriminations between literature and life, romance and novel (where 'novel' equates to 'life' because it is more 'probable', and therefore closer to it). But consider this example of Catherine blushing, on lifting the lid of the stubborn and mysterious chest:

> Her resolute effort threw back the lid, and gave to her astonished eyes the view of a white cotton counterpane, properly folded, reposing at one end of the chest in undisputed possession!
>
> She was gazing on it with the first blush of surprise, when Miss Tilney, anxious for her friend's being ready, entered the room, and to the rising shame of having harboured for some minutes an absurd expectation, was then added the shame of being caught in so idle a search. (*NA* 144)

Catherine is, and is not, Pandora. Catherine is clearly not Pandora, in that she discovers clean linen, rather than evils; but equally, the reader cannot help thinking of Pandora as Catherine is caught rummaging in a forbidden chest, even if forbidden by nothing more than good manners. The point this light scene makes is that there is no outside to fiction: even in life outside novels, we are surrounded by stories that structure and inflect our experience. As such, fiction/life is a false binary: they are not separable and discrete. The novel teems with examples that make the same point, albeit from different angles. For instance, Catherine is enticed by the prospect of visiting Blaize Castle, which she believes to be an authentic, ancient ruin, when in fact it is a modern pastiche, or forgery. In other words, there is no unmediated or uncontaminated origin or 'nature' available to us, no simple dichotomy between past and present. Another such false opposition might be Bath/Northanger Abbey, which is to say, the modern world of commerce, pleasure, and consumption versus the medieval architecture of the abbey. But, as Catherine discovers, the abbey, too, is a mixture of the old and new, archaic and modern.

Perhaps the last false binary to fall is the distinction between romance and novel. We recall that Henry encourages

Catherine to act as if she lived, not in the outlandish world of romance, but in the probable one of the novel, in which fathers are not wife-murderers. But, in her final reassessment of the General, Catherine emancipates herself from Henry's way of thinking in order to assert the synthesis of volume II. She does not maintain that the General is a Montoni (the antithesis to Henry's thesis); but she does believe that, in moral terms, he is not much better. In effect, Catherine has learned to read figuratively. Romances may be 'overdrawn', but they contain their own metaphorical truths: Montoni's representation may not tell us much about the way real fathers actually behave, but it may convey something deeper about common familial tyranny or patriarchal rapacity. In comparison with Catherine's final, measured, 'figurative' reading of the General's character, Henry's earlier defence and censure now seem bland and overly literal: probability, and the novel, too narrowly understood, can itself be fallacious. To use Richard Whateley's terms, Henry has not been philosophical enough in his understanding of the probable.[13]

The synthesis of the novel, then, is that life is more complex than simple binaries suggest – more a matter of greys and ambiguities, of Romance *and* Novel. In recent years criticism of *Northanger Abbey* has, to a degree, polarized. One might crudely characterize the opposing views by saying that one side sees the General as truly a Montoni, a damaging patriarchal figure whose presence throws Henry's tutelage of Catherine into a sinister, repressive light. The opposing argument would be that Catherine learns to discriminate between the General and Montoni, and that this education is innocently advanced through Henry, who, in many respects, speaks for the author. My own view would fall somewhere in the middle between these extremes. However, the point I really want to make is that such a divergence in critical opinion is sustained by the delicate poise of Austen's point of view.

SENSE AND SENSIBILITY

Broadly speaking, in *Northanger Abbey* Catherine has three voices: the language of exaggeration she learns from Isabella;

the language of Gothic romance she first imbibes under Isabella's mentoring, but which is subsequently strengthened by Henry's pastiche, which she is too naive to understand ironically, and which she immediately reproduces, via free indirect speech, in the course of her Northanger explorations; and the language she learns for herself, albeit with Henry's encouragement, which she painfully constructs out of her own experience and knowledge. In the first two instances others ventriloquize through Catherine in a clearly recognizable way, linked to the novel's burlesque purposes. In Austen's subsequent novels, we largely hear the third kind of voice, which is to say, the independent voice of the character, uninflected by comic types. Austen deploys free indirect speech as a means of articulating the voices of her heroines, so that we see things as they do. But these voices do not emerge at once, or in the same way: their emergence, rather, is part of the drama and meaning of her narratives.

This is certainly true of *Sense and Sensibility*. We are only slowly drawn into Elinor's consciousness. The story begins satirically. Quickly and efficiently Austen blocks out her themes. She unfolds her genealogy of the Dashwoods, together with the property complications that set the plot in motion. Two kinds of binding contracts are set in opposition to each other: the binding contract that is property law, where, without specific jointures, property is concentrated through the male line, with a wife's property being swallowed by her husband's through marriage (the story of John Dashwood's aggrandisement); and the binding contract of a verbal promise. It is through such a promise that Elinor's father seeks to protect the interests of his wife and daughters. In effect, good will is set against institutional bias. The feebleness of good will in such a confrontation provides the occasion for Austen's satire as she unpeels the greedy hypocrisy of John Dashwood and his wife.

'Sense and sensibility' are presented to us not as a strict binary opposition but as a pairing in which meanings overlap and blur, as we can see through the middle term both words share: 'sensible'. Another ambiguous dyad might be used to describe the novel's first volume: property and propriety. The terms are filtered through direct, or free indirect speech. John Dashwood repels thoughts of his own stinginess, as regards the disbursement of property, by believing that he 'conducted himself with propriety in the discharge of his ordinary duties' (*SS* 5); Elinor worries over Willoughby 'slighting too easily the forms of worldly propriety' in his conversation with Marianne (*SS* 43); Elinor tells Colonel Brandon that she believes that Marianne's 'systems' of thought 'have all the unfortunate tendency of setting propriety at nought' (*SS* 49); while Marianne justifies her acceptance of Willoughby's gift of a horse on the grounds that it would be a greater 'impropriety' to do so from her brother (*SS* 52). The narrator does not endorse the concept of propriety, or tell us what it is: rather, we see contested versions of it, as characters employ 'propriety' and its cognates to think through their own or others' actions.

We eventually arrive at yet another sense of 'propriety'. An outing is planned to 'see a very fine place twelve miles from Barton, belonging to a brother-in-law of Colonel Brandon, without whose interest it could not be seen, as the proprietor, who was then abroad, had left strict injunctions on that head' (*SS* 54). In the course of the opening volume 'proprietor' comes to stand to 'propriety' and 'property', as 'sensible' does to 'sense' and 'sensibility'. The run of meaning is carefully orchestrated. Prior to the mention of the expedition to view Colonel Brandon's bother-in-law's property, Elinor had been quizzed by Mrs Jennings over her secret love object. The immature Margaret nearly discloses Elinor's feelings for Edward. Elinor and Marianne clearly feel it is a matter of great impropriety to have Elinor's love interest gossiped about, a view clearly not shared by Mrs Jennings or Sir John Middleton. And so might the reader, except that earlier on Mrs John Dashwood had warned Mrs Dashwood against Elinor setting her cap at Edward or his property. Elinor's interest in Edward, if made public, could be easily construed by others – and certainly by the John Dashwoods and the Ferrars – as evidence that Elinor does indeed have eyes on the Ferrar fortune. Elinor had earlier worried about the impropriety of Marianne frankly revealing her feelings towards Willoughby. Through Margaret's clumsiness Elinor is now threatened with the appearance of the same impropriety, one that threatens her prospects of marriage, and by that fact, property.

Volume I sets the scene – the field of action – for Austen's heroines, part of which is the shadowy relationship between 'sense and sensibility' and 'property and propriety'. Schematically, Elinor and Marianne, as 'sense' and 'sensibility', must negotiate their way through the perils of propriety towards property. Austen ensures that we identify with her heroines: she invests them with 'personality'; she invites righteous indignation on their behalf, as we witness the odious John Dashwoods depriving them of what is morally theirs; and she surrounds them with grotesques with whom it would be impossible to identify. As mentioned earlier, 'sense and sensibility' are a constantly threatened binary. Elinor and Marianne are shadowed by two pairs of sisters who uncomfortably double them. Lady Middleton is propriety without sensibility; while Mrs Palmer is sensibility without any sense. By comparison, we understand that Elinor and Marianne are not unalloyed representatives of the antithesis. The Steele sisters are an even more discomfiting echo, but the pairing works in a quite different way. The vast difference between Miss Steele and Marianne serves to desynonymize the two; spontaneity without Marianne's Romantic ideology merely results in Miss Steele's heedless candour. The relationship between Elinor and Lucy Steele operates in the opposite direction: where there is initially difference, we find – if only for a moment – sameness.

Although volume I establishes Elinor and Marianne as Austen's heroines, the only real subject position made available to the reader – the only simulacrum of a personality with which the reader might identify – is Elinor's. Although free indirect speech is periodically employed in volume I as a means of accessing the views of most of the characters, only in Elinor's case is it used to register a thoughtful or considered response. In comparison, Marianne's impetuosity takes her in a comic direction, such as in this reflection, registered through free indirect speech, on Colonel Brandon's reaction to her playing the pianoforte:

> He paid her only the compliments of attention; and she felt a respect for him on the occasion, which the others had reasonably forfeited by their shameless want of taste. His pleasure in music,

though it amounted not to that extatic delight which alone could sympathize with her own, was estimable when contrasted against the horrible insensibility of the others ... (*SS* 30)

The comic exaggerations are Marianne's. It is not simply that Elinor's responses are more measured; it is that being measured is also a matter of being open, and fair, with others. The artless Marianne is without Elinor's 'address': but it is through her address that Elinor displays sensibility towards company. As such, Elinor is the obvious moral centre of the novel.

Elinor's near identity with Lucy Steele thus comes as a shock to the reader. The whole episode is delicately managed through free indirect speech; indeed, through it we can begin to see how the management of point of view is a constitutive element of the novel's meaning. The Steele sisters are introduced towards the close of volume I. Free indirect speech is used to unfold Elinor's thoughts and perceptions, as she is immediately drawn to, and repelled by, Lucy.

When their promised visit to the Park and consequent introduction to these young ladies took place, they found in the appearance of the eldest who was nearly thirty, with a very plain and not a sensible face, nothing to admire; but in the other, who was not more than two or three and twenty, they acknowledged considerable beauty; her features were pretty, and she had a sharp quick eye, and a smartness of air, which, though it did not give actual elegance or grace, gave distinction to her person. – Their manners were particularly civil, and Elinor soon allowed them credit for some kind of sense, when she saw with what constant and judicious attentions they were making themselves agreeable to Lady Middleton. (*SS* 103–4)

It is possible to interpret the language following 'soon allowed' as Elinor's, as her sardonic response to the Steele sisters' 'judicious' sycophancy. The ironic use of 'sense' both allows and repudiates kinship with Lucy, like Elinor, the more 'sensible' of the two sisters. Elinor believes she sees through Lucy: 'Elinor was not blinded by the beauty, or the shrewd look of the youngest, to her want of real elegance and artlessness' (*SS* 106). Owing to this perceived difference, Elinor feels no desire to meet the Steele sisters again. In the final act of volume I, Lucy drops her bombshell, when she confesses her

79

engagement to Edward Ferrars while extracting a promise of secrecy from Elinor.

Volume II opens with Elinor in crisis. It also begins with an extended foray into Elinor's mind through free indirect speech, the first sustained example of its kind in the novel. It is a testing period for the reader as we see matters through Elinor's stressed, unreliable, perspective. She believes that she had 'done nothing to merit her present unhappiness' and was consoled by 'the belief that Edward had done nothing to forfeit her esteem' (*SS* 118). We soon learn that the same cannot be said of the flirtation between Marianne and Willoughby, a flirtation that uncomfortably doubles Elinor's and Edward's. To what extent is Elinor equally incautious in her openness to Edward, as Marianne is to Willoughby? More to the point, where is the dividing line between Edward making love to a woman other than his fiancée, and Willoughby's version of the same thing? Elinor's convictions run counter to the evidence developing around her.

If the failure of Elinor's percipience provides one kind of test for the reader, her moral failure represents another, more exacting kind. 'Much as she had suffered from her first conversation with Lucy on the subject, she soon felt an earnest wish of renewing it; and this for more reasons than one' (*SS* 119). Elinor's reasons are teased out through an unreliable tissue of free indirect speech. Elinor wants to find out as much as possible about the state of the relationship between Edward and her rival; she also cannot 'deny herself the comfort of endeavouring to convince Lucy that her heart was unwounded' (*SS* 120). Elinor protests to herself that she was 'firmly resolved to act by [Lucy] as every principle of honour and honesty directed . . .' (*SS* 119–20). It soon becomes manifest that Elinor is dishonest with herself on at least two counts: rather than endeavouring to ascertain the state of the engagement for Edward's sake, she does so for reasons of her own; and rather than wishing to convince Lucy of her unwounded state, as simple policy, she acts out of *amour propre*. Virtually the last words of volume I inform us that Elinor was left 'mortified, shocked, confounded' by Lucy's revelation. In ways Elinor herself does not quite understand, she seeks to 'confound' Lucy in return, and, as a consequence, adopts her rival's knavish tricks.

The scene of combat is the appropriate one of a drawing room, with Marianne providing cover through her solipsistic piano playing, with the rest of the company distracted by cards. Austen could easily have arranged it for the rivals to meet in private, but as courtship was unavoidably public – as the novel repeatedly insists through the constant gossiping about real or imagined love affairs – so it is appropriate that the rivals in love should have to joust in the public space most commonly associated with marital negotiation. Elinor artfully breaks the ice; with equal address, Lucy thrusts once more towards Elinor's vulnerability, by insisting that she had 'offended' Elinor, which is to say, guessed Elinor's attachment to Edward. Lucy warns her rival off while glorying in her ascendancy. In repelling Lucy, Elinor sacrifices her candour and openness: ' "Offended me! How could you suppose so? Believe me", and Elinor spoke it with the truest sincerity, "nothing could be farther from my intention, than to give you such an idea" ' (SS 123). Elinor equivocates. It is true to say that Elinor had no intention of giving the impression of being offended; it is also true to say that she was, indeed, as Lucy well knows, offended. 'Truest sincerity' is, in this respect, a very complex locution. It appears to be authorial comment rather than free indirect speech. However, it is not a phrase an Austen narrator would ever employ straight. Such a palpable misuse of words is reserved almost exclusively for shallow characters, such as Isabella Thorpe, who, in a like instance, 'promises faithfully'. Truth, like sincerity, does not admit of degrees. 'Truest sincerity' is thus a self-defeating solecism. It alerts us to the fact that, in playing Lucy at her own game, Elinor puts her sincerity at risk.

Elinor's animus against Lucy is evident in the adverbial phrase 'her little sharp eyes full of meaning' used to qualify Lucy's assurance to Elinor that there really was 'coldness and displeasure' in Elinor's behaviour, which is to say, evidence of Elinor's pain. The phrase echoes the narrator's initial description of Lucy as having 'a sharp quick eye' (SS 102). The injection of 'little' transforms the description by drawing in overtones of the predatory or feral, as if Lucy were a cat taunting its prey. In this instance of free indirect speech ('little sharp eyes') Elinor 'others' Lucy. And yet the reader can see how the Dashwoods and Steeles mirror each other, as pairs of sisters similarly situated, both being hard pressed by the dismal reality of husband hunting unfurnished with money. Of course the narrative pulls away from this uncomfortable moment of doubling, where the heroine and the minx appear almost one. As the story progresses, Lucy proves to be the hard, self-seeking, vindictive flatterer Elinor takes her for. And yet it is a dangerous moment for Elinor, as it puts her sincerity at risk. In fact, sense and sensibility may be understood as different versions of sincerity. For Marianne, sincerity resides in spontaneity: first impulses, like first loves, are the truest ones. For Elinor, sincerity is to be found in considered judgement. Both sisters learn that 'sincerity' is not so simple. But sincerity is also what sets the sisters apart as marriageable young woman, apart not just from each other, but from the other women in the novel. Sincerity is a key aspect of their personalities that attracts their husbands. Love's giddiness does not threaten Elinor, but love's rivalry does, as it draws her into insincere and false forms of behaviour.

Sense and Sensibility is Austen's most schematic novel. No other book of Austen's is so systematic in its arrangement of pairs, doubles, contrasts, or reversals, and not just through the device of multiple sisters: for example, Willoughby's behaviour doubles Edward's, while Colonel Brandon's story of Eliza echoes the adventures of the Ferrars brothers. As we have seen, these complications serve to undermine the simple opposition of the title, just as the experience of them deepens the understanding of Elinor and Marianne. But the novel is also schematic in another way. In volume I Elinor is largely on the margins, as the centre ground is taken up with the parsimony of the John Dashwoods, the move to Barton, and Marianne's affair with Willoughby. Elinor's acquaintance with Edward, at Norland, is far less prominent. Volume II takes us much more into the mind of Elinor, partly as a consequence of her rivalry with Lucy, and partly as a result of her anxious attendance upon Marianne in the wake of her split with Willoughby. In volume III, Elinor is back on the margins as the narrative concentrates on Marianne's illness and Willoughby's expiation. The reader yearns for a happy resolution for the heroine, but her own interests are placed to one side, as others' interests crowd the centre. The resolution does, of course, come, but when least expected, with Edward's arrival after the equivocal news of Lucy's marriage to Mr Ferrars. Through this structure, Austen gives emotional substance to a cliché: still waters run deepest. Through her composure, and through her disinterested self-representations, her family mistake Elinor for 'still waters'. Even the reader has not been made privy to the depths of Elinor's feelings, as the period in which we are shown her heart, through free indirect speech, is the one in which she dissembles in order to disarm her enemy. The depths of her feelings are made manifest only in the moment in which they 'burst', with Edward's explanation: 'She almost ran out of the room, and as soon as the door was closed, burst into tears of joy, which at first she thought would never cease' (SS 305). Ang Lee's adaptation of the novel catches the full drama of the moment very well: it is not simply that up until now Elinor has kept her feelings closely guarded; she has kept them closely guarded in a social context in which the expression of a woman's feelings – as regards love and marriage – is fraught with peril, as the novel has previously made us aware, in numerous ways.

PRIDE AND PREJUDICE

More than any other of Austen's novels, *Pride and Prejudice* would seem to fit Lionel Trilling's description of the novel of manners as a form in which a contrast between a middle class and an aristocracy throws manners into relief as 'the living representation of ideals and the living comment on ideas'.[14] But, if *Pride and Prejudice* assents to the view that we know each other through manners, it also complicates it by allowing that manners mislead as much as they inform. Thus Elizabeth and Darcy stare at each other, in initial incomprehension, across a class divide in which Darcy's manners bespeak an unspeakable pride in rank, to Elizabeth, while Elizabeth's are prejudiced by the vulgar family surroundings in which they appear. Darcy and Elizabeth learn to understand each other better, and in this respect *Pride and Prejudice* is also the novel that best evinces Austen's generic interest in moral education. The learning curve, while undergone by both protagonists, is disclosed to us solely through Elizabeth's point of view and here free indirect speech is essential. Whereas we only see the effects Darcy's learning produces (effects mediated and muddied through Elizabeth's limited consciousness), we live through Elizabeth's. Austen is a realist in these matters: her characters do not learn at once, but slowly, in fits and starts. Free indirect speech is once again an essential device, for it is through it that we remain caught, if not stuck, within Elizabeth's misprisions.

The novel is structured around Darcy's two proposals. After his first attempt and rejection he writes a long letter to Elizabeth justifying his actions with regards to Wickham, Bingley, Jane, and the disgraceful behaviour of some members of the Bennet family. Elizabeth finds his explanations, if not his manners, which she still regards as 'proud and repulsive' (*PP* 170) compelling:

> She grew absolutely ashamed of herself. – Of neither Darcy nor Wickham could she think, without feeling that she had been partial, prejudiced, absurd.
> 'How despicably have I acted!' She cried. – 'I, who have prided myself on my discernment! – I, who have valued myself on my abilities! who have often disdained the generous candour of my sister, and gratified my vanity, in useless or blameable distrust. – How humiliating is this discovery! – Yet, how just a humiliation! – Had I been in love, I could not have been more wretchedly blind. But vanity, not love, has been my folly. – Pleased with the preference of one, and offended by the neglect of the other, on the very beginning of our acquaintance, I have courted prepossession and ignorance, and driven reason away, where either were concerned. Till this moment, I never knew myself.' (*PP* 171)

The narrative immediately sets about establishing that self-knowledge is not so simple. First, Elizabeth comes to know herself through knowing Darcy, and one might add, vice versa, which is to say, the self does not exist in isolation, but through social relation. Secondly, the self Elizabeth comes to know is not fixed, but mutable: the self she knows at the end of the book is different from the one she would have known at the start. And, third, the self is, in any event, a fiction. David Hume's sceptical remarks on the fictional nature of subjectivity were widely known in the eighteenth century. Hume argued there were no necessary connections between the causes and effects we habitually linked together. Such links were convenient fictions. Just so the self: the bundle of causal narratives we categorize, collectively, as a unitary self are fictive, for they rest on imaginary connections. Understood properly, the self was no more than a discontinuous series of discrete sense impressions. Such a proper understanding is the peculiar province of sceptical philosophers: the rest of us take recourse to the mythic unity of subjective agency that nature, and culture, furnish us with. Whether or not Austen came into direct contact with Hume's ideas, she certainly understood their substance.

Pride and Prejudice explores all three points. I will take the second – the self's mutability – first. Shortly after her moment of 'self-knowledge', Elizabeth dwells on 'Mr Darcy's letter'. We are then launched into free indirect speech. 'His attachment excited gratitude, his general character respect; but she could not approve him; nor could she for a moment repent her refusal, or feel the slightest inclination ever to see him again' (*PP* 175). Elizabeth's self has already shifted its ground: in ways she does not yet understand, she has developed affections, the first filaments of attachment, to Darcy, which her free indirect speech reveals to us, principally through the direction of her thoughts. She is mortified by her younger sisters' giddiness: 'They were ignorant, idle and vain' (*PP* 175). 'Anxiety on Jane's behalf was another prevailing concern', as her sister had been deprived of an advantageous situation in life 'by the folly and indecorum of her own family!' The reader may reasonably infer that Elizabeth is also thinking, unconsciously, of the even more advantageous position she has been deprived of through the same means. Unknown to herself, her desire, and its motivations, have already altered.

The reason we may surmise this involves my first point, that we know ourselves through others. It is Mr Bennet who raises the relevant point. Elizabeth has been fretting that Lydia's planned expedition to Brighton will further embarrass the family in the eyes of the world, thus jeopardizing Jane's (but also Elizabeth's) marriage chances. Mr Bennet brings her up short with this: 'Do not make yourself uneasy, my love.

Whenever you and Jane are known, you must be respected and valued; and you will not appear to less advantage for having a couple of – or I may say, three very silly sisters' (*PP* 190). Mr Bennet makes the case for intrinsic, as opposed to extrinsic, value: of inner worth versus reputation. As the boundaries between the two kinds of value are permeable, this is a partial truth, although no less valid for being so. It is also the ground of Elizabeth's refusal of Darcy: she spurns him, for esteeming extrinsic values over intrinsic ones, in Jane's case, as well as her own. Unconsciously, and unknown to herself, she has since moved towards Darcy's position, of regarding value extrinsically, just as, and equally unknown to herself, Darcy has moved on to her ground, as he, in his turn, takes Elizabeth's strictures to heart. The fact that he does so leads directly to Elizabeth's future misprisions, where she misunderstands Darcy's actions in involving himself in extracting Lydia from her disgrace: in coming to understand Elizabeth's intrinsic value, he sets himself defiantly against the world. In a sense, in moving towards each other's previous positions, they pass each other by, forming more misunderstandings that await the final clarification. The key to this movement, already present in the stretch of free indirect speech we looked at a moment ago, is made evident to us in the sentence that inaugurates it, which also implicates my third point: 'Mr Darcy's letter, she was in a fair way of soon knowing by heart' (*PP* 175). As she knows it by heart, so her 'heart' changes. And what she knows is Darcy's fictional representation of himself, his letter: she comes to know, and through knowledge, comes to love, Darcy, as he explains, and 'fictionalizes', himself. But to say the self is a fiction is not to say that it is false, for all selves are fictions: and, as fictions, they witness the overlap, the intertwining, of intrinsic and extrinsic values.

All this is subtly and adroitly laid before us in another narrative skein of representation and free indirect speech. In the novel's denouement Elizabeth responds to Jane's enquiry of how long she had loved Darcy: 'It has been coming on so gradually, that I hardly know when it began. But I believe I must date it from my first seeing his beautiful grounds at Pemberley' (*PP* 301). Jane believes Elizabeth is not being serious in saying this, but the joke conceals a kernel of truth, one aspect of which is the glamour of Darcy's material possessions, which Austen is too unsentimental not to acknowledge: hence the device of having Elizabeth speak truer than perhaps even she realizes. If we return to the scene in which Elizabeth first visits Pemberley Woods, in the company of the Gardiners, we gain further insight into the nature of this truth:

> Elizabeth's mind was too full for conversation, but she saw and admired every remarkable spot and point of view. They gradually ascended for half a mile, and then found themselves at the top of a considerable eminence, where the wood ceased, and the eye was instantly caught by Pemberley house, situated on the opposite side of a valley, into which the road with some abruptness wound. It was a large, handsome, stone building, standing well on rising ground, and backed by a ridge of high woody hills; – and in front, a stream of some natural importance was swelled into greater, but without any artificial appearance. Its banks were neither formal, nor falsely adorned. Elizabeth was delighted. She had never seen a place for which nature had done more, or where natural beauty had been so little counteracted by an awkward taste. They were all of them warm in their admiration; and at that moment she felt, that to be mistress of Pemberley might be something! (*PP* 201)

One might deduce from this that the origins of Elizabeth's affections really were mercenary. The balance of the final sentence, which Elizabeth's 'delight' warrants us to read as free indirect speech, would support such a thought. One might summarize its gist as: the social gaze represented by her relatives' approval signifies a highly desirable identity, which Elizabeth now finds appealing. But, in another respect, it signifies the fact that Elizabeth has moved onto Darcy's grounds, figuratively as well as literally. That is, what she finds herself responding to, and warming towards, is Darcy's extrinsic values, which Elizabeth is beginning to read as an index of inner ones. The cue to this reading lies in the landscape. As mentioned before, landscape design was highly ideological at this time. Pemberley signifies a proper care of the estate, which is presented to the reader as conspicuously unostentatious. As we saw with Mr Knightley's custodianship of Donwell Abbey, caring for the estate, and fulfilling one's social obligations, were inseparable activities within the terms of Tory ideology. Darcy's care bespeaks an eschewal of luxury and artifice, of self-regarding consumption: his grounds display the invisible, because seemingly natural, virtues of a proper nurture. In other words, the grounds are another representation of Darcy, are a narrative in which extrinsic values denote intrinsic ones.

The first impression generated by the grounds is then supported by the testimony of the housekeeper, who tells Elizabeth and the Gardiners that Darcy 'is the best landlord, and the best master ... that ever lived' (*PP* 204). Austen furnishes Mr Gardiner with the deflating thought that this is no more than the touching naivety of a devoted servant, but Elizabeth 'listened, wondered, doubted, and was impatient for more' (*PP* 204). Elizabeth, it seems, is beginning to fall in love, not through trafficking with the real Darcy, but through her engagement with his reputation, or 'representation', a development brought to a head with the survey of his 'likeness':

> There was certainly at this moment, in Elizabeth's mind, a more gentle sensation towards the original, than she had ever felt in the height of their acquaintance. The commendation bestowed on him by Mrs Reynolds was of no trifling nature. What praise is more valuable than the praise of an intelligent servant? As a brother, landlord, a master, she considered how many people's happiness were in his guardianship! – How much pleasure or pain it was in his power to bestow! How much of good or evil must be done by him! Every idea that had been brought forward by the housekeeper was favourable to his character, and as she stood before the canvas, on which he was represented, and fixed his eyes upon herself, she thought of his regard with a deeper sentiment of gratitude than it had ever raised before; she remembered its warmth, and softened its impropriety of expression. (*PP* 205)

This run of free indirect speech may appear artless, or natural, but it actually constitutes a dense, supple weave of meaning. The first sentence may seem odd as it locates sensation not where we expect to find it, in the heart, but in the mind. One could say that Austen merely recapitulates the 'sensational' paradigm of late-eighteenth-century psychology, where 'ideas' are first and foremost mental sensations.[15] What this oddness really does, however, is sensitize us to the notion that the seat of emotion is in fact metaphorical, or fictional, and may be located as firmly in one bodily organ as in another. Secondly, it breaks with the gendered paradigm whereby women were understood to love through their emotions, rather than through their 'minds'. And, finally, it alerts us to the fact that Elizabeth is falling in love with an imaginary Darcy constructed out of the social relations she understands as defining him. For Elizabeth, desire, and the ideal of duty, are inextricable. Marks and paint on canvas come alive for Elizabeth to the degree that the likeness is suffused with her imaginary construction of Darcy, where Darcy's construction is fundamentally a matter of his extrinsic values, of the network of moral relations that define him: 'brother, landlord, master'. She is, in turn, caught within the returning gaze or 'regard' of this construction as the object of its desire; and, with this recognition, her own desire, or 'sentiment' (and it is important that we maintain the balance between the two) warms. She has not only been constructing Darcy, but her construction of Darcy has in turn constructed her: she now begins to see herself, and understand herself, in relation to this fictional self. To put it another way, she has herself invested significantly in the male gaze that elicits her desire. Darcy's is not a stock male gaze, but one that Elizabeth has collaboratively constructed through dialogue with what she knows of Darcy's visible relations. Accordingly, we may say that her desire for Darcy is represented to us as a reciprocal process of mutual regard. The paragraph ends with a significant syntactic ambiguity: the 'impropriety of expression' may be understood to refer to the style of Darcy's proposal, or to the facial expression of the painted likeness. The syntax prefers the first interpretation, where Darcy's 'regard' would refer to his former professions of love. But the second sense is also available to us, in which case 'regard' would refer to the gaze of the painted likeness (or the remembered gaze of the person the picture recalls), of which Elizabeth, through projection, now feels herself to be the subject. In both cases, the outward impropriety – whether of verbal or facial expression – 'softens' as Elizabeth learns to connect outer with inner value. 'Every idea that had been brought forward by the housekeeper was favourable to his character':

the phasing effortlessly brings all these senses together: 'character' as reputation or extrinsic value; as personality; as a fictional entity; and as a token of the signifying devices on which such an entity rests.

It is important that we realize that this representation of Elizabeth's growing regard for Darcy is couched as free indirect speech, that we understand that what we encounter is something internal, and interior, to Elizabeth. As such, it cannot withstand the shock of reality, which comes upon her immediately, when the real Darcy turns up, plunging her into 'shame and vexation. Her coming there was the most unfortunate, the most ill-judged thing in the world! How strange must it appear to him! In what a disgraceful light might it not strike so vain a man' (*PP* 206). This is, of course, more free indirect speech. What Elizabeth does not tell us, but which we can easily infer, is that she feels 'shame and vexation' because she now does desire him and his property. Under the duress of her embarrassment, she falls back on her previous conception of Darcy, that he is 'vain'. A moment before she had moved onto his ground, had come to understand social relation as an index of inner merit; she now relapses back to her first impression, in a defensive move. Darcy, meanwhile, has shifted onto her ground by accepting that intrinsic values ought to take precedence over extrinsic ones. Their ways of imagining each other, and hence their own selves, have changed; but that is not the same as insight. Accordingly, they misunderstand each other. Elizabeth certainly misreads Darcy: 'And his behaviour, so strikingly altered, – what could it mean? That he should even speak to her was amazing!' (*PP* 206). It is through his imaginary representations, his fictional selves, that Elizabeth comes to know 'Darcy': but the human reality yet remains a blank she cannot read. This stutter backwards allows Austen to keep within a sophisticated sense of the interpersonal 'probable' as it unfolds in the social field of knowing. It also heightens the narrative tension, for the reader, too, is left in the dark about Darcy, unless, of course, she has learned to suspect the unreliable information free indirect speech furnishes us with.

MANSFIELD PARK

Reading *Mansfield Park* after *Pride and Prejudice* might very well incline one to believe that Austen has become more serious with age. Not only does *Mansfield Park* feature, in Fanny Price, a priggish heroine, but the novel ends with a sustained bout of moralizing in which the virtuous are rewarded and the wicked punished. The adulterous Maria and the hateful Mrs Norris plague one another in ignominious isolation. Henry Crawford is left forever repining the loss of the inestimable Fanny, while Mary Crawford does much the same for Edmund. Yates is made, not only to recant his passion for 'ranting', but to submit, willingly, to the superior wisdom of the father-in-law he had earlier regarded as 'infamously tyrannical' (*MP* 160). Throughout the long winding-up, the narrator unironically extols the virtues of acting through principle in express opposition to the delusive promptings of self.

But this picture is not quite what it seems. The previous three novels were first conceived, if not written, during the 1790s, and unsurprisingly reflect the concerns of the decade. Published in 1814, *Mansfield Park* emerged out of a quite different cultural moment, one aspect of which was the rise of an evangelical movement within the Church of England, a movement with a wider purchase on mid-Georgian attitudes. One might take Edmund's staunch defence of the profession of clergyman, in the teeth of Mary Crawford's scoffing, as an index of this change, although, as David Monaghan has pointed out, the evidence for a pro-Evangelical Austen is mixed, at best.[16] However, as Anthony Mandal has recently argued, the significant context in which to set *Mansfield Park* is the publishing success of the 'Evangelical novel'. Hannah More's ubiquitous *Coelebs in Search of a Wife* (1808) has some bearing here, but the more significant title was Mary Brunton's *Self-Control* (1811), a best-seller of which Austen was acutely aware.[17]

John Wesley's Methodism had been highly influential in the latter half of the eighteenth century, especially among the poor, on whom it was largely targeted, whereas the middle and upper classes found its stridency and austerity obnoxious. Anglican Evangelicanism had affinities with Wesleyan

Methodism, but it was more of a middle-class movement, often in direct opposition to a 'decadent' aristocracy. It found its focus in the Clapham Sect, its major cause in Abolitionism, and its central figure in William Wilberforce. To an extent it was a carry-over of 1790s political activism, but the constitution it now wanted to reform was the nation's manners.[18] Feminist critics, such as Mary Poovey, have long since drawn our attention to the rise of domestic ideology at this time, where women were allotted the central role of moral reform within the confines of the family. Domestic ideology – summed up in the resonant phrase 'the angel in the house' – empowered women by conceiving of them as the central agent in social change, while also disempowering them by imagining this agency in purely passive terms: women reformed through the power of the moral example it was their destiny to fulfil.[19] The Evangelical novel was the fictional embodiment of domestic ideology, hence Mary Brunton's *Self-Control*, which featured a heroine of super-human virtue, who resists, and so reforms, the aristocratic rake who seeks her seduction. As such it is Pamalesque, with the difference that Brunton is explicit about the transformative power of moral principle.

The affinities with *Mansfield Park*, and Fanny Price, are self-evident. But, as Mandal also points out, there are also significant differences. In her letters – and her references to Brunton's novel are examples of this – Austen repeatedly recurs to her own, more 'probable' art.[20] Part of her probable art is her refusal of simplistic causality. Fanny Price's principled refusal of the rake Henry Crawford nearly results in his reformation; but only 'nearly'. For Austen, principle is not a simple contagion, a scepticism that set her at odds with some of the main currents of Evangelical belief. To the extent that it was about availing oneself of the 'stranger within', Evangelicanism was a recrudescence of the Calvinist impulse in English culture. Calvinism required the subject to monitor her inner self for signs of 'election'; Evangelicanism – as a general movement – urged the subject to open herself to her inner religious impulse, to her better, spiritual self, and therefore to 'conversion'. One looked to the God within, rather than outward to mere religious form, or 'conduct'. But for Austen, the inner self was a delusive court of appeal. In so far as they are made known to us, the promptings of Fanny Price's inner self are largely negative, concerning, as they do, feelings of envy and jealousy. If Fanny succeeds as a moral agent, it is because she clings to fixed principles, which exist outside herself, within the wider religious culture. By the same token, Henry Crawford fails, for Fanny has helped him to understand where his duty lies: with Fanny nearly won, he ought to return to Everingham from Portsmouth and prosecute his plan of reforming his estate by curbing his steward and alleviating the needs of his abused tenants, the landowning equivalent of Edmund's professional approach to the vocation of clergyman. The revelation of duty does not transform Crawford's inner self, nor vice versa: outside of Fanny's immediate sphere of influence, and bereft of principles, he quickly turns recidivist.[21]

Austen differs, then, from Evangelicals – including the Evangelical novel – in having a more complex, or more 'probable', sense of self.[22] In probing this more complex sense of self, *Mansfield Park* carries on from where *Pride and Prejudice* left off. Free indirect speech is once again an instrumental aspect of this complexity, although to see how we first have to grasp the central conflict of *Mansfield Park*. Lionel Trilling best puts his finger on it when he characterizes it as the conflict between personality and principle. By personality Trilling intends several things. Above all else, though, he means one of the most pervasive legacies of Romanticism, one still very much with us: the spirit of individualism, or rage for self. But this introduces us to an immediate paradox. In one respect, this urge is a desire to be different, special, unique. In another, it means to adopt a role, a style, or personality, which, by definition, is something already fashioned. Romanticism is about many things, too many, one might say, and generalizations are always hazardous. But, if it is about anything, it is about the desire to discover the authentic self, a self beyond the one society pre-fashions for us, as a 'prison house'. Thus Romanticism's greatest poem, its epic, Wordsworth's *The Prelude*, details and narrates the growth, the 'organic' germination, of the poet's mind. It is not a smooth process, but one continually haunted by false turnings, unfulfilled promises, and, most alarming of all, by the frequent spectralization of a landscape that otherwise works as a token of the authentic. Wordsworth journeys into nature, as a means of discovering his true self. The sublime promises to vouchsafe the deepest knowledge. But the sublime was also a fashion, a way of packaging nature for tourism, or mass consumption. Wordsworth's quest finds itself haunted by the possibility that in seeking his true self he merely reprises a role already preformed by such fashionable rehearsals of the part as James Beattie's *The Minstrel* (1774).

By personality, then, Trilling means something that is both particular and general; natural and forged; ineluctable and assumed. A contemporary instance of the paradox Trilling means (although, arguably, a debased one) would be the teenager who goes shopping in search of the particular mass-produced style that is truly, and individually, 'her'. Trilling reminds us that this double impulse – of being oneself by putting on style – has its own distinct, cultural history, one rooted in the Romantic period. Trilling argues that Austen's irony and the doubleness of Romantic personality are closely linked. Austen's irony is the mark of her style, her personality, as it derives from her own flair for acting, for ventriloquism, for assuming a role, a feeling for the theatrical, embodied, most concretely, in her unprecedented genius for free indirect speech, where she throws herself into the part of her character. As with Oscar Wilde, one can only express one's genius, and truly be oneself, by wearing a mask. In advancing, on the contrary, the claims of principle, and the model of Fanny Price, with her univocal, dutiful voice, and her refusal to 'act' (*MP* 127), Austen appears to be turning against herself. As Trilling puts it, in *Mansfield Park* we encounter irony at war with itself.[23] Or rather, as I shall argue here, irony is the site of the conflict between personality and principle, which *Mansfield Park* explores.

Austen's central device for this exploration is the complex boundary between her novel and Elizabeth Inchbald's translation of Kotzebue's *Lover's Vows*, the text of *Mansfield Park*'s amateur dramatics. As a play, *Lover's Vows* is a tissue of sentimental absurdities. The dramatic irony of *Mansfield Park* is that the play foreshadows – doubly shadows – the action and the meaning of the novel.

The play's theme is one we have already visited on several occasions, as it was the dominant fictional subject of the 1790s: that is to say, it concerns the clash between children and parents – especially daughters and fathers – over whom they shall marry. I have previously put this opposition in a number of ways: as between 'alliance' and 'sexuality'; aristocratic mores and middle-class aspirations; the family and the individual. It was a politically overdetermined plot, hence its recurrence in the fiction of the period. In Kotzebue's version of it, Baron Wildenhaim seduces and impregnates Agatha, a young woman of humble, though virtuous family, leaving her to bring up their son, Frederick, alone. Under pressure from his family, the Baron abandons Agatha for a dynastic, loveless marriage, of which Amelia is the only issue. Repenting the loss of Agatha, the Baron determines that Amelia will not marry without love. Her suitor is Count Cassel, part rake, part buffoon. But rather than dismiss him, Wildenhaim instructs the clergyman Anhault, Amelia's tutor, to teach Amelia to love the Count. Instead, Amelia, through her own ironic forwardness, apprises Anhault of her love for him. The play opens with the chance encounter between Frederick and Agatha, who is now destitute and starving. Desperate to relieve his mother's needs, Frederick attempts to rob the Baron while the latter is out hunting. Father and son do not know each, and, though the Baron is mysteriously drawn to the young man, he resolves on the death penalty. Amelia discovers the nature of their relation; Frederick is forgiven; overcoming his class prejudice, the Baron marries Agatha, his long-lost love; the Count is dismissed; and Amelia and Anhault are allowed to marry.

Initially, the novel appears to draw a distinction between those who wish to act, and those who do not, between the party of personality and the party of principle, between Maria, Julia, Yates, Tom Bertram, the Crawfords, and Mrs Norris, on the one side, and Edmund, Fanny, and Sir Thomas (in his absence) on the other. The leading irony here is largely dramatic, in that the acting party are unaware of the way the parts they wish to play foreshadow their own, real, future selves. They are unaware, because they lack self-knowledge. Julia has become very angry, as Maria has been Henry's choice to play Agatha, a part affording numerous opportunities for embracing:

'Do not be afraid of *my* wanting the character,' cried Julia with angry quickness; – 'I am *not* to be Agatha, and I am sure I will do nothing else; and as to Amelia, it is of all parts in the world, the most disgusting to me. I quite detest her. An odious, little, pert, unnatural, impudent girl. I have always protested against comedy, and this is comedy in its worst form.' And so saying, she walked hastily out of the room, leaving awkward feelings to more than one, but exciting small compassion in any except Fanny, who had been a quiet auditor of the whole, and who could not think of her as under the agitations of *Jealousy*, without great pity. (*MP* 114–15)

There are a number of ways of interpreting this: Julia inadvertently tells us the truth about Mary Crawford, who is to play Amelia, speaking a truth about her the narrator could not directly tell us; Julia projects her jealousy of Maria onto Amelia's character, telling us what she really thinks of her sister; or, thirdly, it is an act of projective identification, in which Julia projects onto Amelia/Mary/Maria aspects of her own flirtatious character she cannot otherwise acknowledge. Significantly, only Fanny feels empathy for her, which brings about another irony if we grant the premise that empathy is the ground of acting, as only the resolute non-actor feels any. Finally, the penultimate, emphatic phrase invites us to consider it as free indirect speech, where Fanny feels, because she knows the agonies of jealousy all too well.

The acting party, then, appear not to know themselves, and not knowing, fail to perceive the affinities between their parts and their characters. Thus, in playing Agatha, Maria rehearses her own future as an abandoned, infamous woman. Rushworth has no inkling of how he really is Count Cassell. The clever, ironic, self-conscious Mary Crawford doubtless knows the ways in which she is Amelia; her misfortune is that she does not know how to step outside the part: she loses Henry, because she cannot stop being Ameliaesque at crucial times.

Having set up this opposition, Austen then undermines it. Edmund is the first to fall. He reproves Mary Crawford for entreating him to play Anhalt by saying 'It must be very difficult to keep Anhalt from appearing a formal, solemn lecturer; and the man who chuses the profession itself, is, perhaps, one of the last who would wish to represent it on the stage' (*MP* 121). The problem is not simply that, in saying this,

Edmund appears to be a 'formal, solemn lecturer'. More significantly it begs the question of what the difference is between representing the profession on stage and in the pulpit. The boundary between life and theatre begins to blur. It blurs further when Henry gives in for patently self-deceiving motives and plays Anhalt, thus rehearsing his future, abortive courtship of Mary.

Sir Thomas's stalwart opposition to acting is also complicated through irony. Unaware, as yet, of the true extent of his children's amateur dramatics, Sir Thomas opens the door of his room, to discover himself, unexpectedly on a stage and next to the declaiming Yates:

> He stept to the door . . . and opening it found himself on the stage of a theatre, and opposed to a ranting young man, who appeared likely to knock him down backwards. At the very moment of Yates perceiving Sir Thomas, and giving perhaps the very best start he had ever given in the whole course of his rehearsals, Tom Bertram entered at the other end of the room; and never had he found greater difficulty in keeping his countenance. His father's looks of solemnity and amazement on this his first appearance on any stage, and the gradual metamorphosis of the impassioned Baron Wildenhaim into the well-bred and easy Mr Yates, making his bow and apology to Sir Thomas Bertram, was such an exhibition, such a piece of true acting as he would not have lost upon any account. It would be the last – in all probability the last scene on that stage; but he was sure there could not be a finer. The house would close with the greatest éclat. (*MP* 152–3)

Drawing back from his part, Yates truly acts when he plays himself. This overlapping of social and dramatic roles also affects Sir Thomas's standing in two, equally devastating ways.

The first concerns the novel's allusions to the West Indies and slavery. The major reference occurs in a conversation between Edmund and Fanny, the context of which is Sir Thomas's new-found pleasure in Fanny's company and Fanny's reticence in engaging him in conversation:

> 'But I do talk to him more than I used. I am sure I do. Did not you hear me ask him about the slave trade last night?'
>
> 'I did – and was in hopes the question would be followed up by others. It would have pleased your uncle to be inquired of farther.'
>
> 'And I longed to do it – but there was such a dead silence.' (*MP* 165–6)

97

The silence has been read as a sign of the embarrassment – the unspeakability – of the slaving wealth that underlies Mansfield Park.[24] But, as Brian Southam points out, by Edmund's account, Sir Thomas is keen enough to talk about the issue: there is silence because the others are bored or indifferent towards Sir Thomas, and are anyway inclined to regard Fanny's interest as hypocritical. Moreover, the internal dating of the novel (Crabbe's *Tales in Verse*, mentioned in chapter XVI, help us pin down the novel's action to autumn 1812), and the historical dates of the abolition of the slave trade within British territory (1807, with a period of grace extending to 1808) make it likely that Sir Thomas is engaged in the West Indies because he is dealing, willingly, with the consequences of abolition. That is to say, Southam reads the scene as evincing how Fanny and Sir Thomas position themselves around the great, 'middle-class', Evangelical mission of the decade, the abolition of slavery.[25] An equally significant aspect of the reference is that it alerts us to Sir Thomas's social position. The political and ideological point about Mansfield Park is that it is an estate without land. Its wealth derives, rather, from the West Indies, from a particularly compromised form of capitalist endeavour. However, yesterday's West Indies projectors are today's gentry. The second and third generations bought themselves facsimiles of age-old estates, and often, as in the Bertrams' case, a title.[26] It is not simply a matter of 'new money'. The point, rather, is that from the perspective of Tory ideology such properties are shams, are, so to speak, theatrical representations of a country estate, for, unconnected with the land, with the networks of responsibilities and duties that accrue to a landowner, who exists as the head of an interdependent community, the house can mean nothing: its social significance has been hollowed out. The ownership of such a house is an expression of personality, an affect of self, an expression of what we would now call a 'lifestyle'. It is emphatically not an authentic social role embedded in ancient customs and practices. It is, from such a perspective, a monumental act of theatre.

Sir Thomas's sudden and unexpected appearance on a stage within his own house reveals the truth of his false consciousness: false, that is, to the extent that he thinks of himself as a Knightley, as the proprietor of an 'authentic' estate embedded within a community. He is revealed as an actor playing a role: that of outraged country gentleman. In both senses of the phrase, Sir Thomas has forged an identity. In so far as the novel proffers a solution to Sir Thomas's ideological plight, it is through the regenerative power of Fanny's attachment to principle, which, as the novel's denouement explains, was wanting in Sir Thomas's upbringing of his children: it was the mere outward form of duty, unenlivened by principle's true spirit, or, indeed, by 'empathy'. However, the novel eschews the simple notion that regeneration is possible through the linking together of letter and spirit, which is where Austen parts company with the Evangelicals. Austen's more complex vision takes us back, once more, to *Lover's Vows*, which cuts both ways. The actors fail to recognize themselves in the play, but so do the non-actors.

Which bring us to the second way in which Sir Thomas's position is undermined. If Sir Thomas had allowed the play, he would have witnessed a representation of his own predicament as well as the hard lessons he eventually learns. The Baron's encouragement of Count Cassel reprises Sir Thomas's tolerance of the foolish Rushworth, while the Baron's opposition to Anhalt marrying Amelia replicates Sir Thomas's initial, unreasoning hostility to Fanny. Austen clearly does not believe that art is powerful enough to pierce the illusions of self-love, unaided. But it is also equally clear that as a novelist she does subscribe to a qualified version of the critical bromide that art is the mirror of life. These qualifications presumably have much to do with Austen's sense of the probable, of which irony is an indispensable aspect. So, while it would be wrong to suggest that Sir Thomas would have been spared his painful mistakes if he had only viewed, and learned from, *Lover's Vows'* version of his errors, it is equally true to say that the novel embraces, rather than disputes, the power of art. The young people have certainly taken unwarranted liberties in their plans for their amateur dramatics; but Sir Thomas is equally culpable in his stiff refusal to entertain the prospect. Sir Thomas's startled discovery of himself on stage is emblematic of his narrow views, of his want of irony.

Fanny, too, is finally compromised by the novel's exploration of the blurred boundary between 'life' and 'theatre', principle and personality. Edmund attempts to humour her into marrying Crawford: 'She feared she had been doing wrong, saying too much, overacting the caution which she had been fancying necessary . . .' (*MP* 293). In being herself, Fanny throws herself into a part, including the role of caution and timidity. Fanny, too, acts.

If acting is a form of mimicry, of adopting another's voice, the greatest actors in the novel are clearly Mary and Henry Crawford. Henry is the best amateur performer and reads Shakespeare beautifully. However, the consummate actor is Mary, who is a past master at turning the words of others. To put it another way, she is the novel's great ironist. She is, in fact, highly reminiscent of the characters Austen had formerly endorsed, such as Henry Tilney or Elizabeth Bennet. She is also very much like *Mansfield Park*'s narrator, who is also a brilliant mimic. If we return to the scene in which Tom Bertram witnesses his father's accidental appearance on stage, we see immediately that it is represented to us through Tom's free indirect speech.

Throughout the novel irony is principally achieved through the narrator subjecting her characters to mimicry. The narrator's ironic, mocking voice is with us from the first words of the novel:

> About thirty years ago, Miss Maria Ward, of Huntingdon, with only seven thousand pounds, had the good luck to captivate Sir Thomas Bertram, of Mansfield Park, in the county of Northampton, and to be thereby raised to the rank of a baronet's lady, with all the comforts and consequences of an handsome house and large income. All Huntingdon exclaimed on the greatness of the match, and her uncle, the lawyer, himself, allowed her to be at least three thousand pounds short of any equitable claim to it. (*MP* 1)

Like *Pride and Prejudice*, *Mansfield Park* begins with the narrator impersonating the community's communal voice, and what this voice tells us is that the folk of Huntington understand social matters entirely in terms of what Thomas Carlyle would shortly call the 'cash nexus'. The narrator cruelly mimics the shallow materialism of the community's conventional wisdom (a wisdom that takes in its stride, as some critics argue, trade in slaves as well as supernumerary daughters).[27] In doing so, she sets the scene for Fanny's 'evangelical', reforming, presence.

Hence the conflict at the very heart of the novel's form. On one side we have a narrator whose greatest affinities appear to be with the party of 'personality', with Mary Crawford, above all; and, on the other, the univocal example of Fanny Price, the resolute non-actor. Through the mimicry of free indirect speech the narrator is able to deepen and complicate her themes and yet appears to do so in direct opposition to the novel's moral centre. One aspect of this complication is the erosion of the ground on which that 'centre' rests: Fanny's naive belief in a fixed, principled self, with a clear line separating life and theatre. And yet the novel appears to end by unironically endorsing the possibility of a principled self, as if the insights of 'personality' were of small moment. In other words, in Trilling's phrase, we find irony at war with itself.

Trilling's telling, historical point is that we are at ease with irony, with the shifting, ludic self: it is unironic moral seriousness that disturbs us. Without wanting to dissipate the challenge *Mansfield Park*'s ending offers us – its apparent resolute opposition to Romanticism – there is a way to read the novel in which the inconsistencies diminish. To begin with, the novel teems with other voices, with the free indirect speech of its many characters, in which Fanny's is an unobtrusive presence. As the novel develops, Fanny's voice comes to the fore: increasingly, she dominates the narrator's employment of free indirect speech. The narrator begins the novel with something like Mary Crawford's sophisticated, mocking irony. Despite indulging herself with the occasional feeling of superiority towards her naive heroine, the narrator ends the story largely in agreement with her and with her voice. So one way of construing the novel's contradiction is that the narrator herself goes through a process of education, in which she learns to forgo the glamorous pleasures of personality – of irony – as she comes to appreciate the value of principle.

EMMA

The denouement of *Emma* nearly founders on the rock of Mr Woodhouse's opposition, his dislike and fear of change. Fortuitously, a gang of poultry thieves have moved into the neighbourhood, a menace that quite overcomes Mr Wood-house's opposition to the marriage between Emma and Mr Knightley. 'Mrs Weston's poultry-house was robbed one night of all her turkies ... Pilfering was *house-breaking* to Mr Woodhouse's fears. He was very uneasy; and but for the sense of his son-in-law's protection, would have been under wretched alarm every night of his life' (*E.* 464). Andrew Davies's screenplay for the BBC adaptation of *Emma* enlarges the event, so poultry stealing both introduces and concludes the narrative. As a revision it is both astute and misleading. Astute, because it successfully foregrounds *Emma's* persistent allusions to the forces that threaten the pastoral stability represented by Highbury's social microcosm, of which Donwell Abbey is the unobtrusive centre. Mr Woodhouse thinks of these threats as house breaking, as the rupture of the domestic space in which true security, and therefore felicity, is found. The departure of Miss Taylor, from his perspective, is one form of house breaking, the invasion of the gypsies who threaten Harriet virtually another. But these are not the only forms of domestic disruption in the novel. In fact, the more we look at it, the more threats we discern. As the illegitimate daughter of a city merchant, Harriet Smith is something of a class cuckoo; the fraternizing of Robert Martin and John Knightley in Brunswick Square is just the kind of promiscuous mixing Highbury (through its guardian, Emma) defines itself against; while the ascendancy of Mrs Elton signals a temporary ascension of the vulgarizing principle. To put matters in this way is also to remind ourselves of what a social alarmist Mr Woodhouse is, for, as revolutionary forces go, these threats are small beer. One might say that, for Mr Woodhouse, change – history itself – is problematic. Andrew Davies's adaptation nicely catches the tone of Mr Woodhouse's fussy paranoia, but it is misleading in so far as it fixes the threat to Highbury as the presence of a largely quiescent 'class' antagonism. For the real threat to Highbury – as I mentioned earlier – is Emma herself, and not house-breakers, poultry-thieves, gypsies, or even tenant far-mers, who, like Robert Martin, riding on the crest of historically high prices for corn, promise to supplant that section of the gentry, such as the Woodhouses, who have stepped aside from the growth economy to repose on diminishing assets.

The real threat to the community is Emma's snobbery. Perceiving this is a challenge for the reader as we mostly view the world through Emma's free indirect speech and therefore through the medium of her faulty values. Emma reflects on the presumption of Mr Elton's proposal:

> But – that he should talk of encouragement, should consider her as aware of his views, accepting his attentions, meaning (in short), to marry him! – should suppose himself her equal in connection or in mind! look down upon her friend, so well understanding the gradations of rank below him, and be so blind to what rose above, as to fancy himself shewing no presumption in addressing her! – It was most provoking. (*E.* 113)

In Austen's early novels – in *Northanger Abbey* and *Sense and Sensibility*, especially – Austen often imparts a satiric twist to her deployments of free indirect speech, so that we know that the narrator dissents from what is being said. In her later novels, the narrator's delivery – her ventriloquism – is more apt to be deadpan. The attentive reader will nevertheless pick up the irony that Emma is similarly blind to the gradations of rank above her:

> Perhaps it was not fair to expect him to feel how very much he was her inferior in talent, and all the elegancies of mind. The very want of such equality might prevent his perception of it; but he must know that in fortune and consequence she was greatly his superior. He must know that the Woodhouses had been settled for several generations at Hartfield, the younger branch of a very ancient family – and that the Eltons were nobody. The landed property of Hartfield certainly was inconsiderable, being but a sort of notch in the Donwell Abbey estate, to which all the rest of Highbury belonged; but their fortune, from other sources, was such as to make them scarcely secondary to Donwell Abbey itself, in every other kind of consequence; and that the Woodhouses had long held a high place in the consideration of the neighbourhood which Mr Elton had first entered not two years ago, to make his way as he could, without any alliances but in trade, or any thing to recommend him to notice but his situation and his civility. (*E.* 113–14)

Like any snob Emma mistakes status for value. Her thoughts unravel her reasons for believing that she is of high status, and Elton of low. The novel, on the contrary, is concerned with value, not status, and in its vision of value Donwell Abbey stands pre-eminent because it is harmoniously interlinked with the community, or 'neighbourhood'. As mentioned earlier, land is the key to this interlinking, as it involves the proprietor in a network of mutual obligations. As a mere 'notch' in Donwell, the virtually landless Hartfield is of limited consequence. The fact that Hartfield's incomes derive from mysterious 'other sources' symbolically links the Woodhouses to the 'city', to cash, and to the likes of Harriet Smith and Mrs Elton. Even on its own terms Emma's snobbery scarcely stands up, for the gentry (and even the middle classes) were riddled with the 'younger branches of ancient families', for that is what primogeniture did: it ensured that younger sons intermingled with the wider, and 'lower', world. From the perspective of strict genealogists, such as Lady Catherine de Bourgh, 'younger branches of ancient families' were doubtless ten a penny. In the very act of expatiating on how Mr Elton fails to notice how much she is his superior in 'fortune and consequence', Emma demonstrates her own inability to appreciate the gap between Hartfield and Donwell, and that is because she goes by the outward marks of status (size of house; income; relations) and not by the value of what these things signify. In terms of the values the novel cares about, Hartfield is indeed a mere 'notch' in Donwell.

Although the narrative is full of ironic hints, noticing them is left as a test for the reader: 'The Coles had been settled some years in Highbury, and were very good sort of people – friendly, liberal, and unpretending; but, on the other hand, they were of low origin, in trade, and only moderately genteel' (E. 171). One can tell by their outrage that many of Austen's democratically inclined American readers believed this to be Austen speaking. That they are, rather, the callow thoughts of an unworldly teenager is evident, not simply from the fact that Austen elsewhere expresses approval of 'low origins', 'trade', and the 'moderately genteel', but from the untenable drift of Emma's thoughts. The narrator notes the Coles' increasing wealth and rising consequence, in part owing to 'the house in town' which 'had yielded greater profits' (E. 171). Emma continues: 'The Coles were very respectable in their way, but they ought to be taught that it was not for them to arrange the terms on which the superior families would visit them. This lesson, she very much feared, they would receive only from herself; she had little hope of Mr Knightley, none of Mr Weston' (*E*. 118). She has very little to hope of Mr Knightley and Mr Weston, because they have better judgement. As earlier noted, Mr Knightley's task is to integrate new money, such as the Coles, into the community. The unexpected profits from their townhouse is another indication that the historical reality of the growth economy crowds in upon Highbury's pastoral world. Knightley's flexibility absorbs the threat, whereas Emma's stiffness augurs friction. More to the point, Emma proves herself to be a very bad neighbour, as when she learns, to her chagrin, that everyone save her has been invited to the Coles' soirée. In excluding her the Coles do no more than she herself wishes. Indeed, she works herself up into believing an invitation from the Coles a 'presumption' and an 'insult', and regrets only that her refusal of the invitation, when it comes, will lack sufficient cutting force. When it does not arrive, the narrator follows Emma through the mental contortions that soon have her reconsidering her position. Although this is once again represented tacitly, through Emma's own words, the cycle of hauteur, mortification, and volte-face is naturally satirically tinged.

Less easy to deal with, however, are these thoughts of Emma's, when, in a more serious mood, she contemplates the attractions of Donwell Abbey – a moment when, as with Elizabeth Bennet, her affections for her destined lover quicken through a perusal of his extensive grounds: 'Emma felt an increasing respect for it, as the residence of a family of such true gentility, untainted in blood and understanding' (*E*. 296). Given that these thoughts anticipate her conversion to Mr Knightley, and all he stands for, they possess a certain gravitas: they appear to belong to, not just Emma, but the narrator, and therefore to Austen. For the modern reader the concept of 'untainted blood' is likely to prove troublesome. It offends against values that are deeply embedded in modern consciousness: against notions of democracy, and, more disturbing still, against beliefs in racial equality. Indeed, for the modern reader the phrase uncomfortably echoes, ideologically, some of the worst excesses of the last century.

But such a testing will occur only if the reader has been inattentive to the use of voice within the narrative. As mentioned earlier, through free indirect speech we are plunged into Emma's perspective from the novel's first sentence. It is not until chapter 20 that we arrive at a sustained alternative. 'Jane Fairfax was an orphan, the only child of Mrs Bates's youngest daughter' (*E.* 136). With the introduction of Emma's rival, a rival voice intrudes. It is not only dispassionate and uninflected with Emma's consciousness, but adopts very different values. For example, consider this representation of Jane's upbringing among the Campbells: 'Living constantly with right-minded and well-informed people, her heart and understanding had received every advantage of discipline and culture' (*E.* 137). We learn of Jane's 'decided superiority' to Miss Campbell 'both in beauty and acquirements'. We also hear of her 'higher powers of mind'.

Within the book the reigning abstract noun for Jane's mixture of natural beauty and acquired culture is 'elegance'. 'Jane Fairfax was very elegant, remarkably elegant; and [Emma] had herself the highest value for elegance' (*E.* 139). In comparison to Jane, Emma lacks elegance; she might have equal beauty, but she possesses less acquired culture. 'Why she did not like Jane Fairfax might be a difficult question to answer; Mr Knightley had once told her it was because she saw in her the really accomplished young woman, which she wanted to be thought herself . . .' In terms of status, Emma surpasses Jane, just as Hartfield rivals Donwell; but in terms of 'value', she is Jane's inferior. We are back within Emma's free indirect speech, and, as it unfolds, we easily spy that Mr Knightley is right about her reasons for disliking Jane: she is jealous of her rival's superior elegance.

Emma might console herself with the notion that her blood is superior, because less tainted, than Jane's, who is related to the lowly (even if newly low) Mrs Bates. But the narrator who at the start of chapter 20 intrudes into Emma's run of free indirect speech clearly does not concur: Jane is superior by virtue of her 'elegance', her superior 'discipline and culture'. I do not think one can extrapolate from this that Austen really is of the democratic party, or is a crypto-modern in her sensibilities. But I think one can say, from the cumulative evidence of Austen's writing, that she is meritocratic. She believes in an equality of merit (even as merit is left an ideological cipher). Thus the estimable Mr Gardiner converses on terms of equality with Mr Darcy, while the comparatively low, such as Elizabeth Bennet, Fanny Price, or Elinor Dashwood, deservedly rise through merit, through 'beauty and acquirements', and through 'superior powers of mind'.

There are effectively two voices in Emma: Emma's, related to us through free indirect speech, and the narrator's, which intrudes only rarely, but which we hear in the description of Jane Fairfax. One is snobbish, the other meritocratic. If one wishes one can read one voice as being more authoritative than the other; alternatively, one can read the novel as a dialogue between the two.

4

Nationalism, Gender, Class

As mentioned in the Introduction, critics of Austen have frequently complained that there is something unreal about Austen's highly polished miniatures: that, despite their naturalistic sheen, her novels lack reality. In a letter to Thomas Hardy from 1913, Frederic Harrison provides an excellent specimen of this view:

> She was a heartless little cynic was Jane, penning satires about her neighbours while the Dynasts were tearing the world to pieces, & consigning millions to their graves. A relation of hers even was guillotined in 1793, her brother was in the fleet that fought at Trafalgar – & not a breath from the whirlwind around her even touched her Chippendale *chiffonier* or *escritoire*.[1]

As I said at the beginning, critics have sought to counteract this view by inserting Austen into her time, demonstrating her engagement with the 'whirlwind', either through her positive involvement in debates about religious renewal, Tory politics, the Regency crisis, and the changing literary scene brought about by the advent of the professional woman writer; or negatively, by voicing visible silences, as regards, for instance, the slave trade, or the scandal of her own relatives dangerously near the turbulent centres of power.[2]

The present chapter is my own essay on how one might position Austen's work within her period, which is to say, within history, within the currents of Georgian change. I have already said quite a lot about this, in passing. For instance, the pastoral is a highly ideological mode, and in her use of it Austen reveals herself to be alert to the changing political scene, as in, for instance, the difference between *Emma* and

Persuasion. I have also referred to Austen's strong sense of the pervasiveness of luxury and consumption, which since the eighteenth century had been the stock language for expressing anxiety over modernity.[3] And, finally, I have referred to the density of Austen's semiological observation, her deployment of 'manners' (as Lionel Trilling argued the case) as a form of anthropological 'thick description'. My aim in this chapter is to pull these strands together.

The way I propose to do that is to situate all three within the history and theory of nationalism, as advanced by Ernest Gellner, in *Nations and Nationalism* (1983) and *Nationalism* (1998). In these books, Gellner sketches out the now commonly held, and commonly contested, view of nationalism as a modern construct.[4] Rather than a necessary expression of human nature, or the ideological product of late enlightenment thinkers, Gellner argues that nationalism was the outcome of a very specific set of recent historical circumstances. Gellner's beginning definition is fairly straightforward: 'Nationalism is primarily a political principle, which holds that the political and the national unit should be congruent.'[5] The transition from agrarianism to industrialism gave rise to the principle. According to Gellner, agrarian society was 'Malthusian', a zero-sum game, and consequently hierarchical and socially inert.[6] A horizontally integrated minority at the top of the social pyramid sought to maintain its status through a monopoly of high culture, through the knowledge of, and therefore possession of, the kingdom's sacred scripts. Below this top layer was the peasantry, atomized into so many separate villages or clans. The notion that government and state, culture and 'nation', should be congruent was alien for the peasant, as it was for the priest or courtier. Industrialization altered everything by decisively breaking the Malthusian laws of agrarianism. For the first time in history, governments survived on the basis of delivering constant growth. In the 'growth' economy, the political dynamics change completely. To begin with, the growth economy is fundamentally based on the free flow of information. In industrial societies, 'high culture' (meaning access to complex literacy) becomes the norm, and education 'universal'. Maximizing access to high culture involves social mobility and a weakening of kinship ties in favour of ones defined by vocation (exo-socialization). In the industrializing process, 'cultures' and political boundaries tend to coalesce into single, homogenous entities, or nations, and they do so because it is economically advantageous: it facilitates growth. These historically new social formations coalesce into separate pools, as the lay of the land – variations in geography, language, and ethnicity – determines.[7] There is economic competition between these various polities. It is this competition that gives rise to national self-consciousness, and, with it, to nationalist ideologies.

Gellner's hypothesis, then, provides us with four key points. First, nationalism 'is a theory of political legitimacy'.[8] Secondly, it comes to fill the gap created by the erasure of the Divine, which had underwritten earlier versions of state legitimacy. It follows that nationalism is a modern ideological construction, which directly leads to the third point: nationalism is always an expression of false consciousness. As Ernest Renan famously observed, 'getting its history wrong is part of being a nation'.[9] Alternatively, one might say that nationalism and the heritage industry are part and parcel of the same process of historical amnesia and nation building. The general aim of nationalist ideology is to create a myth of unitary national origin, whereby the present 'congruent' polity is understood to be the manifestation of an ancient culture. Nothing must contradict this narrative, including, or, indeed, especially, evidence of past diversity, heterogeneity, and conflict.[10] In Gellner's view, nationalism is not just a profound version of false consciousness, it is a complete overturning of reality: whereas nationalism likes to see itself as the ascendant expression of an ancient 'low' or peasant culture, in fact it is almost always the imposition of high culture on the low, at the latter's expense.[11] The fourth point is the dating of the emergence of nationalism, and its ideologies, in the eighteenth century. E. J. Hobsbawm reads nationalism as coming to fill the void created by the crumbling of traditional paradigms of state authority. Between 1789 and 1815 few long-established regimes 'had not been transformed ... Such traditional guarantors of loyalty as dynastic legitimacy, divine ordination, historic right and continuity of rule, or religious cohesion, were severely weakened ... all these traditional legitimations of state authority were, since 1789, under permanent challenge.'[12]

110

What relation has this reading of the origins of nationalism with Austen? For a start, it provides a very clear picture of Austen's historical moment. Once one begins to see Austen as an observer of the 'permanent challenge' mentioned by Hobsbawm, a recorder of the minutiae of life, which in their turn register what is 'in the air' – those intangibilities that concretely shape modern life – then so we see Austen's texts as fairly swarming with contemporary references. To take an obvious example, consider the issue of vocation. Lionel Trilling observed that one of the aspects of the life recorded by Austen, which must seem remote to the modern reader, is the fact that so many of her personages have nothing to do, except be: their identities are not shaped by work, but by rank and caste; not by professional activity, but by leisure.[13] As a couple of nineteenth-century American commentators put it, with some asperity, 'the normal activity of human beings is virtually excluded, and all the characters are parasitical beings subsisting upon the labour of others in a cloistered and subdued lotus-land free from the gusts of hunger and passion.'[14] This may be so, but Austen is at least accurate. The numbers of thousands with which brides are endowed or gentlemen enriched – and the various degrees of comfort and luxury these thousands generate, at 5 per cent interest per annum, in government bonds, issued to fund the war effort – are calculated to a nicety. So accurate, that V. S. Pritchett was moved to observe that Austen should be thought of as a war novelist 'formed very much by the Napoleonic wars, knowing directly of prize money, the shortage of men, the economic crisis and change in the value of capital'.[15]

More to the point, Austen's parasitical gentlemen are only part of the picture. Austen always supplies us with contrast. The society she represents is not fixed in aspic; on the contrary, it is depicted in a state of crisis and change. To use the language of Gellner's analysis, Austen presents us with a picture of the old, agrarian order, one thrown into historical chiaroscuro through the presence of telltale signs of the new growth economy. The identities of Austen's characters may be largely fixed within the older agrarian economy, of unchanging status and inherited wealth; but they are identities under stress.

111

This stress is paradoxically registered in Austen's attitudes to gender; paradoxical, because we derive some of our clearest historical clues, not from Austen's imagining of the feminine, but of what it is to be male. Readers may find the glamour of Austen's strong female personalities an irresistible temptation to biographical speculation. In these feisty characters, so wonderfully balanced between irony and contrition, subversion and stoicism, one is tempted to identify something of the author. That may or may not be a profitable line of enquiry. Biographical speculation apart, what I think we can say is that Austen regards the feminine as the self's default state (with a couple of caveats I shall shortly return to). Which is perhaps only to say that it is in men that the politics of gender are for Austen especially clear.

For example, take the case of Robert and Edward Ferrars. One way of regarding Edward is that he bumbles his way through life with a mix of quixotic loyalty and incontinent flirtation. Another is that he finds a way to achieve what he most wants in life: to disencumber himself of his fortune. Edward wants this, because he is in search, not of a life of financial ease (which he has by and from birth), but of masculine self-respect. Accordingly, his prospective fortune is an emasculating threat. As he complains to Elinor, when he fears he shall be uselessly rich, what fitting thing is there for him to do? His fate is amply sketched out for us in the shape of his brother Robert, who is encumbered with none of Edward's scruples. Robert is more than happy to take his brother's place as the heir of his bossy mother's immense fortune. As the proleptic man of wealth, he is also effeminate, with a highly developed sense of sartorial finery and useless luxury.

To recur to Austen's hostile, nineteenth-century American critics, referred to a moment ago, Austen is not blandly neutral to male parasites of the upper classes. She has, on the contrary, decided views. At first glance, they may not seem consistent. After all, Mr Knightley is no less wealthy than Robert Ferrars eventually becomes, and he, clearly, is neither effeminate nor a target for Austen's hostile irony. But that is because Mr Knightley internalizes the work ethic of Austen's Tory ideology. In chapter 3, we saw how this was so: rather than parade his wealth and status, as a means of social theatre, Mr Knightley industriously ensures that the social machine is well oiled by working behind the scenes to integrate the worthy, succour the poor, mollify the aggrieved, and check the wayward. As a symbol of his correct, masculine values, Mr Knightley walks, while his carriage – a potential item of dangerous luxury – is busied in the interests of those less well off than himself, to whom he is, by virtue of his privileges, indebted. Mr Elton, by contrast, is a potential Robert Ferrars. Although he holds the position Austen most often associates with a socially redemptive masculinity, that of clergyman, his snobbery undermines his manhood. If he is not emasculated by his boastful, forward, materialistic wife, he is certainly effaced by her; and, in comparison to Mr Knightley's pedestrian habits, his carriage rides with his wife take on the appearance of effeminate show: effeminate, because show.

The modern reader may find it curious to discover that Austen associates the clergy with manly behaviour, given that for us, conventionally, few vocations are less overtly 'macho'. But that is because Austen associates masculinity – at any rate, its positive forms – with social responsibility and not with physical or amorous prowess. Thus her seducers, Wickham, Willoughby, and Henry Crawford, enter her stories with a masculine swagger as Romantic heroes, but leave them as dependent, isolated, and reduced figures. In their reduction lies their effeminacy.[16] Despite the occasional flight of giddy levity, Henry Tilney is the model of a man, partly because he does the right thing by Catherine and partly because he happily embraces his destiny as a second son bound for a parsonage. As we have seen, this is a destiny Edward Ferrars secretly prefers and one Edmund Bertram openly embraces. Austen does not infallibly see the clergy as models of masculine rectitude, as in, for instance, the unfortunate example of Mr Collins: yet the principle holds good, as Mr Collins has clearly unmanned himself, rendering himself socially useless through his obsequiousness and abject snobbery.

One might easily take Austen's representations of her, if not ideal, then certainly robust clergymen as a depiction of ageless, Home Counties England; but in fact her representations are, historically, sharply inflected. As we saw in the previous chapter, Austen was very much part of a religious revival that distinguished the post-Revolutionary period. Of the wilder shores of country and urban Methodism Austen does not tell us much, but she does seem to have shared the milder form of evangelicalism that then stirred the Established Church. The revival had two related aspects: there was a general feeling that the Church ought to fulfil a role in shoring up the social order lest it collapse into French-style anarchy; and an equal understanding that the Church ought not to be the preserve of the younger sons of the nobility, and certainly not if they continued to regard the profession as no more than a 'living'. Austen's clergyman heroes, and the heroines who marry them, are not above calculating the size of the livings set aside for them, or the lifestyles they might support (and, in opposition to the Evangelicals, they are undisturbed at the prospect of accepting more than one), but they approach their futures in a mood of vocational seriousness. Whereas in a Fielding novel one might expect the vicar to hunt, drink, and swear, while his curate delivered the sermon, it seems unfeasible Jane Austen ever considered such a future for Edmund Bertram or Henry Tilney.

Austen's positive depictions of her clergyman heroes, then, are historically inflected in that they are part of a general, country conservatism that typified much of English life following the radical turbulence of the 1790s and the reaction it provoked. There is also a class dimension to this inflection, in that it is clear that Austen shares the general contempt of the landed gentry for the aristocracy, frequently regarded by the gentry (and there is a provincial/metropolitan animus here too) as improvident, snobbish, and socially irresponsible. Austen in fact includes few aristocrats in her novels; and, if one wanted corroboration of the fact that her characters are largely drawn from what her contemporaries would have called the lower or middling sorts, one need only turn to her critics, who often scarcely mention anything else.[17] Lady Catherine de Bourgh is an aristocrat, as her name obviously denotes, as are Lady Dalrymple and her daughter from *Persuasion*, along with Lady Russell from the same novel, although only through marriage. Sir Walter Elliott, as a baronet, belongs to this side of the borderline between upper gentry and aristocracy, which is why he defers to Lady Russell's judgement, and fawns on the Dalrymples. Generally speaking, Austen's aristocrats are the objects of her contempt, sometimes mild, sometimes not. Darcy is an ambiguous case. A relative of Lady Catherine, he has aristocratic connections on his mother's side, but, as his father was from an untitled family, so is he (*PP* 287). On the other hand, Pemberley's size suggests the estate of a Whig grandee, especially if one reads it as based on Chatsworth, in Derbyshire, the ancestral estate of the Duke of Devonshire.[18] Darcy's manners (as far as Elizabeth Bennet's first glance is concerned) are equally undecided.

Austen's clergymen, then, are in clear contrast with the aristocratic values Austen elsewhere repudiates. One might see this as expression of a tension between the middle class and the aristocracy, which is how Lionel Trilling saw it.[19] But, to an extent, this is a historical solecism. Class, in the modern sense, had not yet come into being. Our modern sense of class draws upon the potential, imaginary identification with others similarly defined by occupation and wealth, upon what Ernest Gellner calls 'exo-socialization'. In the agrarian order outlined by Gellner, this is clearly not possible, for 'occupation' had yet to assume its full, contemporary value within the growth economy. Austen's characters lack a 'class' mentality. What they do have, very acutely, is a consciousness of rank and station. In the agrarian order outlined by Gellner, there may have been a clear line between the elite and the peasantry, but the elite itself was not arrested in a state of immobilized gradation. On the contrary, European elites were distinguished by considerable mobility, as estates, and status, waxed and waned. What was missing from the elite's sense of its own identity was that rank or station had much or anything to do with occupation, with one's profession, with 'work'. Hence Sir Walter Elliot's devotion to the book of books, the *Baronetage*, with its minute registrations of rank and status.[20] Above all else, the *Baronetage* is a record of kinship exchange. On the one hand, the status attached to the exchange of kin (in Sir Walter's terms, the portion of glory merited by his daughters' marriages, and carefully noted in the book) is registered through wealth; on the other, it is independent of it. Hence Sir Walter's confusions. According to his lights, Admiral Croft derives

115

small benefit from either his distinguished profession, or his new-found wealth, as a successful admiral grown rich upon enemy prizes in the war against France. Similarly, Anne's marriage to Captain Wentworth brings only a small increase in status, despite Wentworth's recent prosperity. In this respect, status, as Sir Walter understands it, is independent of wealth. And yet Sir Walter is equally highly conscious – an embarrassment repressed through bluster – that his own status has been placed in jeopardy by his relative poverty. In modern terms, we might say that Sir Walter suffers the ideological confusions of his 'class', of holding values that both acknowledge, and obscure, the material realities that underpin his position.

Gellner would not argue that the old, agrarian order did not feature professions: it obviously did, as Stendhal reminds us in the title of his most famous novel: the 'red' and the 'black', army and Church. These were, after all, the primary destinations of younger sons in a society based on primogeniture. The point, rather, is that this older sense of profession is inflected differently from our full-blown notion of a middle class, with the vast army of professions required to service the growth economy: lawyers, doctors, teachers, professors, civil servants, and businessmen of many (if not all) descriptions. In a state of affairs where the elite went to the army or Church as a matter of course, profession did not signify; or it did not signify so much as the position one held within the network of kinship exchange, as registered in Burke's *Peerage*. Jane Austen, then, may appear to conform with this older agrarian notion of profession, given that her younger sons, almost exclusively, are clergymen or military people. In fact, Austen's understanding of profession is inflected by a new sense of occupation that was emerging as part of the historical formation of the middle class. What she presents us with is not so much a tension between an aristocracy and a middle class, as a tension between two different ways of regarding the professions, or 'work', within the upper echelons of the old agrarian economy. Austen's representation of gender, especially masculinity, once again provides us with the clearest clues as to what these differences are.

Thus, if we return to Mr Knightley, we can see that he is represented as masculine, because he puts his Tory ideology to work, as does Mr Darcy, whereas Sir Walter does not, a failure represented as his effeminacy, a quality expressed as an excessive interest in his looks. His proud boast that his face discloses a more youthful appearance than Admiral Croft's, because not scorched and leathered by the sun, betokens his antipathy to work, to professing his 'class', to undertaking the management of his estate as a socially responsible vocation. His inordinate concern for his reflection, whether provided by a mirror, the *Baronetage*, or Aristocratic connections, signifies, not just the traditionally female vice of vanity, but a ruinous contempt for the value of an occupation in its new, professional sense. Austen draws a clear link between social degeneracy and the old agrarian identification of status with rank. Captain Wentworth, on the other hand, along with Edward Ferrars and Edmund Bertram, are figures of social renewal, not because they are members of emerging, middle-class professions, but because they approach traditional occupations in a new spirit of professionalism. They not only are, but do; and in that serious doing, they realize their masculinity. Other members of their 'class' not invigorated by this spirit of professionalism are correspondingly tinged with effeminacy, such as Mr Collins, who is too supine to perform his duties, or Wickham, who finds himself effeminized through the abject dependency his shiftlessness has reduced him to.

One might thus more correctly formulate Trilling's point by saying that Austen's novels reveal a proto-tension between the traditional values of the aristocracy and the ideology of an emerging middle class, a criss-crossing and overlapping particularly evident in the ideology of the 'gentry' with its multiple affiliations to both poles of this tension. The point of this reformulation is not to adopt a nit-picking attitude towards Trilling's admirable criticism, but to remind ourselves that it is indeed the case that Austen's novels are not suspended in a historical vacuum, out of harm's way from revolutionary whirlwinds, but are, to the contrary, fascinatingly eloquent about their historical moment. It follows that we should not expect Austen to adopt a consistent attitude towards the changing scene she observes. And that is in fact the case. For example, consider *Emma* and *Persuasion*, both 'late' novels, and yet very different from each other. As I earlier

observed, *Emma*, on the face of it, is Austen's most conservative text, one that most fully articulates a Tory ideology that
has been put to work, and made to work. As such, it adopts a
grudging attitude towards new money, either accepting it on
its own, conservative terms, in the case of the Coles, or,
through the obnoxious figure of Mrs Elton, proscribing it as
outside the charmed circle of pastoral happiness, because
beyond (in its associations with slaving Bristol) the inclusive
capacities of Tory idealism. In John Knightley, *Emma* contains
a rare example of a second son who does not pursue the red
or the black, but follows a profession that both looks back to
another ancient profession, the law (with its London inns of
court), and forward to the legal apparatus supporting the very
engine of the growth economy, the financial networks of the
'city'. As a serious man of law, one evincing the new
professionalism, we would expect John Knightley to be presented to us as masculine; but in his peevishness and ill temper
he falls someway short of the masculine ideal realized in the
stoical manners of his older brother. John Knightley is not
exactly effeminate, but neither is he a specimen of robust
manliness. In fact, at times, he is alarmingly like Mr Woodhouse, who, although respectfully treated, is clearly effeminate.
Unmistakably, Mr Woodhouse is (and these are the terms the
novel explicitly invites) an 'old woman'. In terms of our earlier
discussion, this is self-evidently because Mr Woodhouse refuses to shoulder his share of the ideological work as one of
the heads of the community. He is, in other words, the
antithesis of Mr Knightley. One way of understanding John
Knightley's effeminate peevishness is that it is an index of his
deracination: forced to sojourn in the city, he has lost his
connection with 'home' – with an estate embedded within an
organic community – and hence with his identity, the source
of his power and manhood. As a professional required by the
burgeoning of the growth economy, John Knightley is less,
rather than more, masculine than he might have been. *Emma*
both embraces the new spirit of professionalism in its representation of Mr Knightley and repudiates it in its treatment of his
younger brother.

Such ambivalence seems a long way from *Persuasion*'s
forthright version of the overtly masculine professionalism of

Captain Wentworth and Admiral Croft, who come in to renew Sir Walter Elliott's rotten centre. One might speculate that the difference is owing to the fact that *Emma* is in its outlook a pre-Waterloo text, which patriotically imagines England's traditional social machinery in a state of good working order, as a bulwark against the dangers of French-style innovation, and *Persuasion* a post-Waterloo one that meditates renewal, now the danger is over. Alternatively, one might observe that throughout her career Austen is a writer of different moods; and, in the subtle differences in her generic play, in the modulations of her use of romance and novel, pastoral and comedy, alternative visions are variously advanced. But whether pro- or anti-improvement (remembering that 'improvement' was a buzz word of contemporary political debate), it remains the case that innovation and change permeate the world of her novels.[21]

I earlier said that Austen regards the feminine as the self's default state. By that I meant that Austen's male characters suffer the pressures placed upon gender by a changing world, whereas her heroines exist in a condition of apparent, clear-sighted rationality. I also said that the statement required a few caveats, which I shall now make. First, the state of embodying subjective normalcy extends only to her heroines, and even then, not to all of them (Catherine Morland being the exception). Secondly, this state of clear-sighted rationality is indeed only apparent: her heroines do indeed find their subjectivity – their desire to make room in the world for their egos – pressured by issues attendant upon gender. Thirdly (and this combines the previous two points), these pressures are embodied through other female characters, in whose fate one finds potential reflections of the heroine's condition. Henry James called such characters 'ficelles' – figures who bring out the lights and shades of the protagonist's condition. If Austen's heroines resist the constricting pressures of gendered identity, the female figures around them, the ficelles, generally do not; and in their fates, we read the heroine's principal dangers. Generally, these gendered pressures fall into two main categories: the marriage system; and sensibility.

All readers of Austen know that the great calamity that haunts her heroines is the threat of the spinsterhood that

119

Austen herself suffered. Or rather, they think they know it. Marriage was indeed the great, constraining institution that shaped the lives of young women of Austen's place and time. As comedies of manners, marriage is also what her books are principally about. But I have couched the issue in the way that I have – by suggesting that Austen regards the feminine self as our 'default state' – because I wanted to draw attention to something that is extraordinary in Austen. And that is that Austen resisted the overwhelming cultural pressures of her time to imagine feminine subjectivity in terms that were both gendered and narrowly defined. Before Austen, I think it no exaggeration to say that, in the English novel, female characters largely derive their characterization from gendered templates. It is often said that in 'romance' – and here I mean the kind of archetypal narrative best delineated by Northrop Frye – female figures tend to be treated as extremes, as either impossibly pure or unfeasibly wicked, as vestal blondes or sultry brunettes.[22] By contrast, in the 'novel', by which I mean the invention of what the eighteenth century typically called 'probable depictions of contemporary life', it is perhaps more appropriate to designate this binary as Clarissa/Pamela. Of course Pamela is neither wicked nor impure. If any thing, the reverse is the case; but it is clear that, even as she protests her innocence in defiance of Mr B., she employs the subtle arts of coquetry. Clarissa, by contrast, is stiffly virtuous, as befits her socially superior status. Female characterization, before Austen, was generally filtered through these romance and novel stereotypes. One way of regarding *Northanger Abbey* is that it is a work in which Austen has yet to free herself fully from older narrative models. Thus, although Catherine Morland's character is represented to us as contravening the gendered stereotypes inhering within the concept of a heroine (largely through her tom-boyish proclivities), there is something Pamelaesque in her, in her unconscious employment of coquettish arts (such as her winsome ignorance) that quite conquer Henry.

Susan Morgan puts her finger precisely on the point I mean when she asks the question, 'why is there no sex in Jane Austen?' Her answer is that sexual desire sharply accentuates the gendered roles Austen was trying to resist for her heroines:

in other words, it threatened their capacity to be rational.[23] But, if Austen's heroines escape the subjective deformation attendant upon gender's codifications, her supporting characters, her ficelles, do not. And, as I mentioned earlier, in terms of placing Austen within her period, two gendered concerns particularly stand out: marriage and sensibility.

Entering the marriage market, or system, is a perilous moment for either sex; and in the story of Austen's minor characters we read the reality of these perils for her heroines. Thus Charlotte Lucas, who marries the dreadful Mr Collins out of desperation; society marriages so rickety they barely survive the celebration of the nuptials, such as those in *Mansfield Park*; victims of the marriage system's invidious property laws, such as Mrs Smith; marriages by seduction and scandal, such as Lydia Bennet's; and underlying all, an anxiety to be properly married that is so intense as to be unbearable (best expressed in *Sense and Sensibility*).

However, all these perils, pitfalls and pressures are broadly true of novels dealing with marriage across the tradition of Western novel writing. Where Austen's attitude to marriage is more specifically, historically inflected is in her treatment and support for the ideal of 'companionate marriage'. The phrase has been championed by the English historian Lawrence Stone, who has argued that during the eighteenth century there emerged a new, bourgeois pattern of marriage, defined by the ideals of companionship.[24] Previous patterns of marriage were largely aristocratic, or plebeian. Aristocratic marriage was based on the system of primogeniture, in turn supported through alliances 'arranged', or at least sanctioned, by the family. Plebeian marriage was equally pragmatic. Bourgeois marriage opposed both, through the ideals of romantic love. This may sound as though the middle classes were injecting sexual passion into their concept of marriage, but the real point of romantic love was that it stressed marriage as something freely chosen by the individuals involved, on the basis of a meeting of minds, or personalities. It was, in this sense, companionate, and it represented the triumph of love over family.

Critics have attacked Stone for moving precipitously from propaganda to reality: although the ideals of romantic love and companionate marriage may have been highly touted by bourgeois writers and commentators, it does not follow that middle-class alliances were any less happy or troubled or pragmatic than those of other classes. Stone often draws upon novels for evidence supporting his claims, which may be problematic for historians, but not for us, as the issue is not whether marriage really did change, but whether there was a change of attitude towards it. Clearly, there was, as we can see from even a cursory glance at late-eighteenth-century culture. In the proto-nationalist discourse of Gothicism that emerged at this time, the companionate habits of Gothic marriage practices (where the Goths or Saxons stand as ancestral figurations of Englishness) are explicitly contrasted with those of despotic, oriental nations. As we saw in chapter 1, companionate marriage was an issue that explicitly divided Edmund Burke and Mary Wollstonecraft, with the latter attacking the former's attachment to the degradations attendant upon aristocratic primogeniture. In countless Gothic novels young lovers devoted to the values of romantic love marry across the class divide in defiance of their feudal-minded parents.

Austen, clearly, is equally committed to the ideals of companionate marriage. In Austen there is no sex (at any rate, no overt sex) because in her works marriage is primarily a meeting of minds, rather than bodies; and not because Austen is a Victorian prude in-the-making, but because she vigorously advocates a progressive cause, one placing her closer to Wollstonecraft than to Burke. In Austen, minds are sexy, and bodies 'mental', in that they are semiological constructs the heroine has to 'solve'. Just as Austen imagines a reinvigoration of the Church through its professional reformation, so she supports a renewal of the institution of marriage by imagining unions of love rather than alliances of family convenience. Such a conception of marriage enhanced the dignity of women by granting them the status of spiritual equality, which is how her heroines appear, rather than as glittering objects of kinship exchange, or as bright commodities caught up in the circulations of the economic system. However, it would be wrong to construe this affinity with Wollstonecraft as evidence of lurking radicalism in Austen. Burke may have won the overall argument in his *Reflections on the Revolution in France* – at any rate his defence of constitutional organicism left a powerful legacy – but he most definitely lost the argument over primogeniture and marriage. The historical tide ran, rather, with the rising bourgeoisie and their embrace of the ideal of campanionate marriage, no matter how compromised in reality.

Austen's novels flow along with this tide. Apart from *Emma*, which is militant in its hierarchical pairings, all her novels feature marriages that cross emerging class divisions. Almost invariably social miscegenation is the ingredient she uses to thicken her plot. Part of her remarkable resourcefulness is that she never quite uses the same emerging division twice, with the possible exception of *Northanger Abbey* and *Sense and Sensibility*, which both feature marriages bridging the growing gap between a segment of the gentry that has no capital purchase on the growth economy (and so materially dwindles) and a segment capitally enfranchised. In *Northanger Abbey* Catherine may see, or rather misread, General Tilney as a feudal tyrant, yet his 'mod. cons' attest to his myriad links to the new consumer economy. As we have seen, *Pride and Prejudice* figures a contrast in which offspring of gentlemen (Elizabeth and Darcy) come together across a division that Lady Catherine would have no hesitation as describing as 'middling' versus aristocracy, especially given Lady Catherine's tendency to equate Elizabeth with her lowest relations, which is to say, with the Gardiners and their associations with 'trade'. The later novels are more explicit still about the material realities underlying these emerging divisions. *Mansfield Park* may seem to reprise the plot of successful versus indigent gentry, as advanced by *Sense and Sensibility*, but it is a repetition with a difference. Indigence is now linked to decline into, not genteel shabbiness, but the plebeian, or something like a proto-image of the working-class existence so familiar to us from Victorian fiction. Fanny's family in Portsmouth are on the face of it gentry down on their luck – Fanny's mother having made an incautious love marriage – but their proximity to the 'working-class' bustle of the docks links them to the emerging strata of urban poor from whom the new proletariat will be historically recruited, an association strengthened by the noisome claustrophobia of the family home. Meanwhile, *Mansfield Park* hints at the origins of the Bertrams' prosperous gentility: trade, the empire, sugar, and slavery. In *Persuasion* new wealth literally has its origins in war, as sanctioned profiteering, but the real contrast, as we have seen, is between self-reliant professionalism and a profligate, self-regarding, failed custodianship of inherited wealth. If *Emma* papers over the social cracks emerging elsewhere in Austen's œuvre, such concealments themselves become eloquent when read in the context of Austen's other books.

The narrowness of Austen's social miscegenation, the fact that she mixes classes only subtly distinct from each other, may blind us to the fact that she embraces the historical tide of 'embourgeiosification'. That she does indeed do so is most evident in her support for companionate marriage. The linkage between the two things, companionate marriage and a new, middle-class professionalism, is most evident in Austen's warm portrayal of the Crofts in their carriage. Whereas the vulgar Eltons whiz around in their cabriolet as an intrusive show of wealth (where display appears the only bond cementing the happy couple), the Crofts are more interested in the mutual pleasure they derive from their common pursuits. Their driving style is also drawn to our attention. The Crofts have met Anne and Captain Wentworth on a walk, and are now driving the young people home in their gig:

> '– My dear admiral, that post! – we shall certainly take that post.'
> But by coolly giving the reins a better direction herself, they happily passed the danger; and by once afterward judiciously putting out her hand, they neither fell into a rut, nor ran foul of a dung-cart; and Anne, with some amusement at their style of driving, which she imagined no bad representation of the general guidance of their affairs, found herself safely deposited by them at the cottage. (P. 83)

In an essay on the origins of fable and romance, James Beattie draws a distinction between the way the Goths and orientals treat their women:

> With us, the two sexes associate together, and mutually improve and polish one another: but in Rome and Greece they lived separate; and the condition of the female was little better than slavery; as it still is, and has been from very early times, in

124

many parts of Asia, and in European and African Turkey. But the Gothick warriors were in all their expeditions attended by their wives; whom they regarded as friends and faithful counsellors . . .[25]

Admiral Croft is just such a Goth, and Mrs Croft just such a trusted counsellor: hence the comic portrayal of happy equality where the couple jointly steer their way through a life of professional and domestic felicity.

However, Beattie goes on to say that the Goths also treated women as

sacred persons, by whom the gods were pleased to communicate their will to mankind. This in part accounts for the reverence wherewith the female were always treated by those conquerors: and, as Europe still retains many of their customs, and much of their policy, this may be given as reason of that polite gallantry, which distinguishes our manners . . .[26]

'Polite gallantry' has another name: chauvinism. Cultural historians tell us that the chivalrous attitude towards women, such as that praised by Beattie, was preliminary to a new formation that hardened during the Victorian period. It is referred to, variously, as a new domestic ideology, or as the cult of the 'angel in the house'.[27] According to this ideology, women were not just men's equals, but their superiors as regards sensibility, the capacity to nurture, and the potential for domestic virtue. In other words, it was an ideology that praised women only to lock them more securely in the home. Although one can see the lineaments of this emerging ideology clearly enough during the Georgian period, it is not one that Austen appears to have subscribed to. In any event, in comparison with, say, Dickens, one does not encounter in her works heroines who redeem the home – like Esther Summerson in *Bleak House* – by means of selfless virtue and an insatiable appetite for dusting. The closest Austen comes to endorsing such a view of gender is in her portrayal of Fanny Price. But Fanny's virtues are not exclusively domestic. And while much is made of her ability to inject order into the chaos of family life in Portsmouth, there is an implicit suggestion that her value requires a larger stage than the distaff side of the home.

I earlier said that it is Austen's heroines who represent her sense of a rational norm, a condition I characterized as a default state of subjectivity. In making the claim I distinguished between Austen's heroines, who are in possession of their faculties, and the surrounding ficelles, who bear the marks of the social pressures that define them. Another way of putting the same claim is that Austen's heroines appear to rise above history, whereas her lesser characters are swamped by it. When Emma accompanies Harriet to Ford's, Harriet is busied in shopping in a manner the male characters would have no hesitation in characterizing as feminine: 'Harriet tempted by every thing and swayed by half a word, was always very long at a purchase; and while she was still hanging over muslins and changing her mind, Emma went to the door for amusement . . .' (E. 192). While Harriet dithers, Emma turns her back on shopping, surveying the wider world, in search of intelligence. Exasperated by Harriet's choice neurosis, Emma tried 'with all the force of her own mind, to convince her that if she wanted plain muslin it was no use to look at figured; and that a blue ribbon, be it ever so beautiful, would still never match her yellow pattern.' (E. 194). Emma plays the 'male' role of forcing rational choice in contrast, not just to Harriet, but to Miss Bates, who cannot enter Mrs Ford's Aladdin's cave of consumer desirables without commenting on Mrs Ford's new shipment of ribbons (E. 196). One might argue that Emma adopts a disinterested posture towards shopping because she already has everything; be that as it may, Austen continually draws a contrast between her heroines, who are indifferent towards consuming, at best, and the ficelles and grotesques, who often seem to think of nothing else, unless, like Lydia Bennet or Isabella Thorpe, they are distracted by officers. When Elizabeth and Jane Bennet return home to Meryton after their trip to London, they are greeted by Lydia and Kitty from the window of the coaching inn. Lydia then opportunes her older sisters for money to pay for the lunch they have just improvidently purchased after a shopping trip in which Lydia has bought a bonnet whose main virtue was that there were two or three 'uglier' ones (PP 180). As a silly flirt, Lydia is not the calculating coquette that Isabella Thorpe is, but in other respects Lydia echoes Isabella's characteristic combination of sex, shopping, and stereotypical femininity.

Through her ficelles and female grotesques, Austen embroiders the pressures that deform the female character. As regards marriage, figures such as Charlotte Lucas, Lucy Steele, and Mrs Dashwood illustrate the legal and personal perils that attend upon a system of primogeniture. As regards sensibility, Isabella Thorpe, Lydia Bennet, and Marianne Dashwood illustrate the connections between fashion, consumerism, and the traits of conventional femininity. Or rather, through contrast with her heroines Austen locates the origins of their feminine affectations within the flow of history. In so far as her heroines appear to rise above these pressures – evincing stoicism at the prospect of the insensible suitor and disinterest in fashionable consumption, whether of clothes or manners – so they appear to rise above the currents of history, establishing a kind of heroism in so doing. And yet, as we shall see in the Conclusion, this transcendence is only apparent, at least to this extent: for if Austen's heroines spurn fashionable trivialities, they do so only to embrace values that were equally of the moment.

Conclusion

In my Introduction I raised a series of questions: what is it about Jane Austen's work that has provoked such strong identifications among her readers? Why is 'Jane', the person, the most loved of English writers? And what about her writings identifies her as 'English'? In the previous chapters I have been setting out the various pieces of my answer, but to read them, we will have to stand back, and adopt a different perspective. This perspective comes in two parts. For the sake of convenience I shall call the first a 'print-culture' perspective. The second returns us to the theory of nationalism introduced in the last chapter.

PRINT CULTURE

Until fairly recently, Austen's achievement was understood largely within the terms set by a traditional history of the novel. Ian Watt's *The Rise of Novel* was especially influential. The 'rise' signals an evolutionary metaphor. Inward psychology was introduced by Samuel Richardson, who was followed by Henry Fielding, who pioneered outward realism. The two, in turn, were succeeded by Jane Austen, who married their achievements through her innovative use of free indirect speech, thus paving the way for Henry James.[1] The trouble with this approach is that it rests on a number of unexamined assumptions, such as, for instance, that round characters are superior to flat ones, or that realism is better than fantasy or romance. A print-culture perspective is, contrastingly, value free, at least as far as literary affect is concerned. Another way of putting this would be to say that such an approach is indifferent towards whether it is dealing with quality writing, or with the 'trash' of the circulating libraries. Instead, it considers the history of literary forms as part and parcel of a larger story involving the history of print, the growth in reading audiences, the technological changes that made this growth possible, and the financial and industrial developments that were part of this technological change. It would also include a recognition that the category of 'literature', together with its institutionalization as a canon of classics codified within a discipline taught within schools and universities, are themselves epiphenomena of the growth of print culture.[2]

As is nationalism, which is where we begin to gain a firmer purchase on the questions I have asked. For Benedict Anderson, print makes nationalism possible. In a pre-print culture the community extends no further than the immediate members of the 'tribe' among whom are circulated the stories and myths that imaginatively bind the community together. Print vastly extends the realm of this imagining, with the community or nation extending to the limits of the circulation of the common, printed language.[3] For Ernest Gellner, nationalist ideologies and the expansion of print are at once the causes and the effects of the 'growth economy'.

Nationalism provides us with a firmer purchase, because it alerts us to many of the tensions and contradictions that traversed the reading and writing communities of the late eighteenth century, ones arguably still with us. The eighteenth-century cult of genius provides us with a fruitful, if at first sight unlikely, starting point for understanding the tensions and contradictions generated by a rapidly expanding print culture. Although we tend to think of Romanticism in terms of the rise of the individual, epitomized above all in the figure of the Romantic genius, the figure has, in fact, deep eighteenth-century roots. According to mid-century commentators such as Edward Young, Alexander Gerrard, and William Duff, the genius was original, 'primitive' (in the sense of being close to the 'infancy' of the people for whom he speaks), and natural.[4] Homer was the original genius of the Greeks, while Shakespeare was England's. Eighteenth-century bardolatry may be understood as a nationalist ideology, in which England's distinctiveness and greatness coalesced around its possession of an original genius to rival the ancients, but also, by implication, its continental rivals, frequently understood by the English as lacking their own Shakespeare, which is to say, a poet of Homer-like proportions.[5]

The eighteenth-century cult of genius developed not long after the introduction of the copyright law of 1709. While it is difficult to detect any simple cause and effect, one can say that the introduction of copyright sharpened the issues of originality, plagiarism, and forgery for both publishers and writers.[6] The early eighteenth century was, famously, a period of rapidly expanding print production. Coffee houses and newspapers spread exponentially. Later in the century the first circulating libraries appeared, thus bringing novels and romances within the financial range of an ever-increasing readership. To feed this market, publishers required 'originals', or new product. This raised an awkward question: in literary terms, what was the difference between imitation and invention; allusion and plagiarism; a copy and an original? The premium placed on originality by the book trade coincided with values generated by the growth of nationalism, which was itself a part of the expanding print culture. As we saw in the previous chapter, according to Ernst Gellner, nationalist ideologies are a particularly acute form of false consciousness. That is, whereas nationalism prefers to see itself as the ascendant and legitimate expression of an ancient 'low' or peasant culture, in fact it is almost always the imposition of a modern 'high' culture at the latter's expense. The eighteenth century is full of print-culture episodes that vividly exemplify the force of Gellner's argument. For instance, in 1761–5, James Macpherson, an Edinburgh teacher, published the fragments of a Gaelic epic by the Scottish bard, Ossian. Since the defeat of the Jacobite cause in 1746, the indigenous Highland culture had been systematically repressed and dismantled. Now a member of the high, lowland, print culture, which was complicit in the suppression of the Highlanders, was disseminating in translation the work of an indigenous poet who was to be to the Scottish, Highland nation what Shakespeare was to the English, or Homer to the Greek. Except that Ossian, the Gaelic original genius, was a fake, the product of a forgery, a high cultural fantasy that exploited the oral culture to construct a literary version of an imaginary nation, a nationalist project centred in the salons of Edinburgh. It was also, in simple publishing terms, a roaring success. Macpherson was not alone: many others exploited publishers' needs for copyrightable products of original genius while simultaneously feeding the nation's ideological desire for indigenous works that shadowed forth national legitimacy, appetites they fed through fakery. Thomas Percy's *Reliques*, Thomas Chatterton's Rowley poems, W. H. Ireland's Shakespeare forgeries are all prime examples. Other 'forgeries', such as Herbert Croft's *Love and Madness* (1780) or Horace Walpole's *The Castle of Otranto* (1764), provide more equivocal examples.[7]

The cult of original genius thus exemplifies one of the main contradictions of eighteenth-century capitalism. Capitalism is about the ever-increasing circulation of manufactured goods or 'luxury' items; it also requires consumers willing to purchase them. The works of original genius are luxury items in that we do not need them for personal survival, at least, not literally. They were also very expensive. So why did people purchase them? From a print-culture perspective, one would say that they did so because such objects conferred éclat upon the purchaser, or, to use the word of French sociologist Pierre Bourdieu, 'distinction'. It augmented one's personal value or 'cultural capital' (another phrase of Bourdieu's).[8] Such self-cultivation increased one's individuality or personal distinction. However, at the same time as one is purchasing 'individuality', many others are doing the self-same thing, through the acquisition of identical commodities. Just as Macpherson, Percy, Chatterton, Croft, and Ireland produced works of 'genius' that were both original and forged, so consumers purchased objects that were distinct, yet common.

Jürgen Habermas's hugely influential theory of the bourgeois public sphere provides one answer as to why consumers should invest in artistic luxuries. Habermas divides the public sphere into the literary and the political. For Habermas, the political public sphere comes into being whenever two or more people gather together to talk politics, rationally. Habermas describes his concept as a 'normative ideal'.[9] Some commentators have misunderstood Habermas's phrase as signifying

131

something utopian; in order to clarify his meaning, Habermas has subsequently reclassified his definition as a 'performative utterance', in the manner of, for instance, 'promising'. A performative utterance is not referential but performs its meaning through the act of utterance, as in promising to marry someone. For a promise to be properly performative, a number of conditions must apply, such as the presence of a promiser, a promisee, and the concept of a contract. Just so the public sphere. For two or more people to 'public-sphere', there must be a concept of politics and the belief in the speakers' ability or right to influence political activity through rational discussion. According to Habermas, the public sphere developed in the seventeenth century in opposition to aristocratic forms of publicity that largely turned on the display of status. Hence the design of aristocratic houses, which generally featured courtyards and large public rooms in which 'rank' could be staged. For the emerging bourgeoisie, authority derived, not from received patterns of a religiously sanctioned social and political hierarchy, but from a notion of individual rights. Habermas argues that this new sense of the individual transformed the meaning of privacy, from its older sense of lack, or privation, to its modern associations with individual fulfilment; hence, for example, our customary assumption that it is only through privacy that we can truly become ourselves, that, like Jane Eyre in her enclosed window seat, Thoreau on his pond, or Virgina Woolf in a room of her own, it is only in private that we can forge who we publicly are. The bourgeois household did not revolve around a large, theatrical, public room, but was divided into smaller private spaces conducive to this self-becoming. For Habermas, the emerging bourgeois public sphere was an expression of the private: through the public sphere the bourgeoisie agitated for political changes that would protect its sense of the 'private', the values it attached to individuality, and vice versa, for the value of individuality was in turn used to legitimate the changes the bourgeoisie sought through the public sphere. Hence, too, the importance Habermas ascribes to the literary public sphere, which he understands as an adjunct to the political: for it was through literature, through the eighteenth-century psychological novel, especially, that the bourgeoisie rehearsed and deepened the 'interiority' that was at the heart of its commitment to its versions of privacy and publicity. Habermas's performative corrective was necessary because he was often understood to be saying that the eighteenth-century bourgeois public sphere was restricted to physical sites, such as the French salon or the English coffee house (whereas Habermas wants to argue that one could 'public-sphere' anywhere, provided there were two or more people subscribing to its normative ideal). While restricting the public sphere to particular sites is a misunderstanding, it is an understandable one, given Habermas's particular interest in these cultural institutions, because both perfectly exemplify the congruence posited by his theory: of private and public, the literary and the political. As my discussion of Habermas will have made clear, the bourgeois public sphere was made possible by print, by the proliferation and circulation of novels and newspapers, which were the occasion for the rehearsal of interiority.

Alongside Habermas's theory of the public sphere we can set Michel Foucault's comments on the 'author function'.[10] Foucault reminds us that there are a number of ways in which we might organize and so interpret texts: for instance, through genre, length, format, date, and so on. The author function is simply another kind of classificatory tool. However, it has a particular relevance to us, for to interpret a work by author is to read it as if it were a means of accessing the writer's psychology, her inner self, the quick of genius that lights up her otherwise hidden interiority. One of the consequences of bardolatry was the vogue (still current) of reading Shakespeare's sonnets in this way, as if they were a rebus for the author's life and personality, which we might know, if we could only read them right. As Foucault also reminds us, the 'author function' has not always been with us: it has a history. It is in the Romantic period, in tandem with the cult of original genius, that it especially comes into play. Recent work by print-cultural historians appears to confirm the point. Throughout the eighteenth century, circulating library and publishing catalogues classified books through genre and format: whether they were histories or romances, epics or comedies, and whether they were quarto, folio, or duodecimo. Richard Sher has analysed the catalogues of the publisher

Constable; in 1800 Constable's cataloguing system changes, from genre and size, to author, a move reflected across the industry.[11]

The novel, then, was one of the luxury items that began to circulate in late-eighteenth-century markets in increasing numbers, an object that gave rise to this contradiction: readers read for distinction and individual cultivation, *en masse*. And if we ask, why was the impulse to read strong enough to override this contradiction, we get this kind of answer from Habermas and Bourdieu: because reading novels deepened the interiority that held such a prominent value in the logic of the bourgeois public sphere; and because reading novels put one in touch with – by encouraging identification with – the genius/author who produced it, thus further accruing to one self 'distinction' and cultural capital. Or, rather, one did, if one read the right sort of novels, for the market also encouraged mere facsimiles of 'genius', writing done by formula, as if by machine: in other words (to use the contemporary phrase) the 'mere trash of the circulating library'.

In *The Economy of Character: Novels, Market Culture, and the Business of Inner Meaning*, Deidre Lynch makes one of the strongest arguments yet mounted in favour of what I have a called a print-culture perspective. Her remarks on Austen are particularly suggestive for us. In the late eighteenth century, she argues,

> one reads in a crowd. In the inside stories of the novel of manners, the romantic reader finds the means to sound the depths of her own special self and manifest her distinctive sensibility. In the age of steam-powered printing presses and circulating libraries, however, the silent reader's intimate transactions with the inner meanings of literature are public-spirited in a couple of senses: from such pursuits of individual distinction a public sphere is composed, and such pursuits of individual distinction are haunted by the murmuring spirit of mass consumption . . . Austen registers novel readers' need to navigate ironies of this kind.[12]

Lynch lays out these ironies by revisiting the question of round and flat characters. That is to say, she interprets 'round' characters as the promise of depth, as the fulfilment of Habermasian interiority or of the Foucaultian 'author function', and 'flat' characters as indices of mass consumption, of novels as mere, endlessly reproducible 'product', as 'clichés' and 'stereotypes', where these terms haunt subsequent debate through the repression of this historical fact: 'cliché' and 'stereotype' are printers' terms coined during this very period, buried reminders that the fruits of genius are, in the end, the commercially driven productions of bits of metal on paper.[13]

According to Lynch, Austen did not attempt to resist the tide of mass literature by creating a bulwark of round characters; rather, she represented the ironies inherent in 'reading in a crowd' in explorable form. Lynch cites *Sense and Sensibility* as an example. As we saw in chapter 3, Austen deploys free indirect speech in the novel in order to create a sense of Elinor's hidden depths. Where Marianne acts out the expected role of a jilted heroine by weeping, taking to her bed, and becoming ill, Elinor keeps her own disappointment quiet. Or, rather, she does from her family, but through free indirect speech we are made privy to Elinor's secret thoughts and suffering. For the reader Elinor becomes a talismanic figure of 'depth' or 'roundness' – of full personality – whereas Marianne dangerously skirts cliché through her self-dramatizations: she comes perilously near the stereotype of sensibility. Lynch's point is that Austen's novels repeatedly stage this contrast between mysterious depth and commercial flatness, between heroines who act as an earnest of 'distinction' or 'personality' and characters that recall the figures of mass consumption, including the mass consumed romance. Thus Elinor is not only juxtaposed with Marianne, but the Dashwood girls in turn are set against a series of duplicate sisters who bear all the marks of two-dimensional fashion, or, as Lynch might say, they bear the signs of their stereotypical origins. In *Northanger Abbey* we observe Catherine Morland's struggle with the third dimension. Although she is introduced to us as being instinctively hostile to romance stereotypes through Isabella Thorpe and her own naivety, she repeatedly risks 'flatness' through her susceptibility to fashionable language and commercial literature. In Lynch's terms, Austen plays with the reader's need for 'roundness' – for the cultural capital invested in high status 'personality' – by continually threatening her heroine with cliché, before, in the end, furnishing her with a proper

135

inwardness, an interiority in stark contrast with the flatness of Isabella Thorpe's fashionable commercial culture. Lynch's argument works equally with Lionel Trilling's contrast between principle and personality in *Mansfield Park*. Principle, in Lynch's terms, is the mark of roundness; personality, of 'flatness', of character as it is already predetermined by the commercial book trade, or the popular theatre. The last point may seem counter-intuitive. However, in Lynch's argument, 'real' personality can only be hinted at, and never fully represented, as it is defined – and marked out – by mystery, in the same manner that Susan Price's candidature for Mansfield Park, economic self-sufficiency and full personality, is something simply given, and not explained.[14] Roles, no matter how glamorous, or Romantic, always carry with them the mark of 'done-beforeness', of inauthenticity, of character as commercial product. According to this ideology, one cannot cultivate personality, any more than one can forge 'genius': it simply is, or is not, mysteriously there.

What is it about Jane Austen's work that has provoked such strong identifications among her readers? Lynch provides us with an answer, which is partly to do with Austen's technical expertise in sustaining the illusion of personality in fiction, as analysed in chapters 1 and 3, and partly with the way in which Austen dramatizes the differences between roundness and flatness, personality and stereotyping. Through free indirect speech, Austen invites the reader to identify with the personalities she sets in opposition to antagonistic stereotypes, drawing distinction from their 'depths'. Austen's readers find this attractive, because they, too, experience the cultural contradictions of 'reading in a crowd'. Reading Austen is to feel special, individual, 'distinct', as one loses oneself in the mysteries of her heroine's personalities in direct opposition to stereotypical characters who themselves reprise the commercial and cultural pressures from which Austen's heroines offer release.

Why is 'Jane', the person, the most loved of English writers? The answer here is an extension of the foregoing. She is the most 'loved', because she was the first novelist, and in some ways the most accomplished, to develop the illusion of personality in fiction. In perhaps no other way does Austen so profoundly reveal her connection with Romanticism than in the success with which she glamorized the individual human subject. Moreover, by providing a porous boundary between the spritely and tart narrative voice, and her spritely and tart heroines, with their hidden depths, Austen provided works in which identification with her heroines was also an implicit identification with the author. Thus, although critics as influential as Marilyn Butler and Jerome McGann have questioned whether Austen was Romantic at all, on the grounds that she expressed scepticism if not outright ideological hostility to Romanticism's leading contemporary expressions, such as 'sensibility', it is possible to argue that she is in fact one of the most Romantic of all late Georgian writers: possible, that is, if one accepts the view that the critical institutionalization of the 'author function' is one of Romanticism's most profound and lasting consequences.[15] To say that Austen, the person, is the most loved of English writers is thus partly to say that the public that loves her are deeply and unconsciously committed to the cult of authorship. We love Jane Austen, the person, because we feel that we apprehend Austen's personality through her personalities, who in this reading function as the spectral traces of the Author as genius.

NATIONALISM

Implicit within Q. D. Leavis's statement is the assumption that Austen is loved, because she is English, which takes us to our final question: what is it about her writings that identifies Austen as English? The history of her critical reception is of great interest here, for the fact is, Austen was not initially received as being particularly English at all. There were two, significant, laudatory reviews by Sir Walter Scott and Richard Whateley, both of which argued that Austen was a pioneering novelist of great importance.[16] Most of her other notices were short, and, in so far as they display a common theme, it is to agree that her novels are 'safe', evince naturalism, and describe 'middling' rather than high sorts.[17] The view that Austen was peculiarly English began to come into fashion only after the publication of her nephew's hagiographical memoir, portraying her as a saintly aunt and village stalwart.[18] The memoir triggered a spate of reviewing and retrospection. The trans-atlantic reception that followed also strengthened the percep-tion of her Englishness, as it tended to be a feature her American critics picked out, whether for or against. From our point of view, though, the most significant factor was that Austen began to be sold – and sold in large numbers – as an especially English writer. To understand this aspect of her reception, we need to return once more to theories of national-ism.

One might paraphrase the critical literature on the history of nations like this: nations are inventions, and, like all inventions, they possess a history. Before the eighteenth century, before an expanding press made possible coherent and projective imagin-ing, there were no nations in the modern sense of ethnically and geographically congruent polities. Nor are there any now, for in reality nations are mongrels, are heterogeneous collections of peoples arbitrarily packaged within imaginary borders. And that, for historians of nation building, is precisely the point: nations are ideological constructions in which facts are turned upside down. Whereas nationalist ideologies fantasize that the nation is the ineluctable fruit of a long period of gestation, rooted in homogenous soil, and redolent of the indigenous folk, in reality the nation is the confection of deracinated intellec-tuals, locked in the discursive structures of pastoral, who project onto a 'people' who do not necessarily want it a political project in which the former's interests are sustained through the 'nation', meaning an economically productive entity with a pressing need for intellectuals to imagine its existence.[19]

It is this reading of the nation – the nation as 'contingent discursive construction' – that Slavoj Zizek endeavours to supplement in his essay 'Enjoy your Nation as Yourself!':

> A nation *exists* only as long as its specific *enjoyment* continues to be materialized in a set of social practices and transmitted through national myths that structure these practices. To emphasize in a 'deconstructionist' mode that Nation is not a biological or trans-historical fact but a contingent discursive construction, an over-determined result of textual practices, is thus misleading: Such an emphasis overlooks the remainder of some real, nondiscursive kernel of enjoyment which must be present for the Nation qua discursive entity-effect to achieve its ontological consistency.[20]

Zizek's implicit point is that the passions of ideology, what one might call the energetic investments of false consciousness, are not enough to explain the 'ontological consistency' of the nation, a consistency that produces not only extreme identifications, but extreme acts of violence in their defence. For the nationalist – and we are all nationalists now – the nation is *cosa nostra*, 'our thing', our peculiar and special thing to be defended from an Other who always already desires it, who wishes to enjoy our enjoyment and so purloin the kernel of what we are, the pleasure that we take together, including the pleasure we derive from so taking our pleasure, and that communally defines us.

The psychoanalytical inflections of Zizek's argument pose problems for a historicist perspective, such as ours.[21] Nevertheless I want to hold on to Zizek's identification of 'our thing' as the 'kernel of the *real*' that imparts ontological consistency to the discursive construction of the nation. It is my contention that Jane Austen has become, for the English imagination (the English, and not the Welsh or the Scots, and certainly not the Irish), 'our thing', a sign of the ineffable, which only the English can properly enjoy, an enjoyment that in fact defines the English, as English. When Henry Tilney castigates Catherine Morland in *Northanger Abbey* for suspecting his father of wife-murder, he complacently and ironically boasts of an England that has become the acme of a modern, civil consciousness: it is a place where roads and newspapers lay everything open (so enabling communal imagining, as Benedict Anderson would put it) and where neighbourhoods of voluntary spies ensure the rule of law. Catherine always operates as Henry's parodic foil, garbling what he has to say, thereby revealing what he did not want to utter, or did not exactly mean. So it is when she afterwards rehearses Henry's lesson in her mind. In Catherine's discomfiting version of Henry's nationalist homily, the boundaries of uncivil European Otherness extend beyond the continent, embracing Britain's Celtic fringe, reaching down, even, to northern Britain, to that area of national darkness somewhere beyond the Watford gap (*NA* 174). In other words, in Catherine's parody, England's green and pleasant land is shrunk to the imaginative compass of the Home Counties. In the face of this parody (and in defiance of Austen's irony), Jane Austen has become, not just

139

England's peculiar 'thing', but an England imaginatively congruent with the Home Counties, a congruence that defies the disparateness of Austen's geographical settings.

I earlier referred to Lionel Trilling's last essay on Austen, where he wonders over the enduring attraction of Austen for American undergraduates. That in Austen's world individuals draw their identity from their caste, not from what they do, struck Trilling as a particularly indigestible anachronism. What point of contact could there be between her world and ours where work and identity are so closely linked?[22] Her social remoteness was already a feature of American criticism of Austen.[23] And yet, persistently, Austen is received as one of us.

I began this book with a quotation from Q. D. Leavis asserting that 'it is *only* Jane Austen . . . who is loved and esteemed by her readers as a *person*'.[24] For Leavis, to know Jane Austen is to love her; and what we love is an impression – a spectre – of Englishness. Although not one herself, there is something of the 'Janeite' about Leavis's comment, that strange chapter in the history of Austen criticism where appreciation of Austen's elusive qualities, but especially the rarity of her wit, was the sign of mystic inclusion, of being a member of an exclusive club dedicated to the private enjoyment of England's special thing.[25] The Leavis quotation was approvingly supplied by the more recent critic, Roger Gard, who, after making sport of Austen's more simple-minded nationalist admirers, provides his own, more complex variety: 'Jane Austen is one of the great English writers. She is not simply, along with Shakespeare, or in a different way, George Eliot or Dickens, one of the best writers England has produced; she is also one of the few writers who may be said to define it.' Austen, it seems, defines England. Gard's qualification of his assertion is worth attending to in greater detail:

> This is a reason, to put beside the fineness of her language, for our feeling that Jane Austen is especially, and congenially, English. She writes from and into a spiritual atmosphere which, by means of a positive absence of perceived restraint, is a real presence in English culture and those related to it. Unpolitical, she is therefore the realistic novelist of an evolving national democracy.

Austen's congenial Englishness, appropriately enough, is expressible only through paradox: 'from' and 'into' collapse into the self-same space; an 'absence' becomes a 'presence'; while 'unpolitical' ends up as its obverse. I am not saying that Gard's language is without sense. He means that Austen supported emerging democratic values by depicting characters uninhibited by rank who freely converse across class lines, such as Elizabeth Bennet speaking her mind to Lady Catherine de Bourgh. I am saying, rather, that the pressure of Austen's ineffable Englishness has contorted Gard's language, as if 'our thing' could not be approached save through linguistic genuflections commensurate with its spectral nature.

In Zizek's terms, for Gard, Austen is 'the remainder of some *real*, nondiscursive kernel of enjoyment' that vouchsafes the nation's ontological consistency. For Gard, this 'kernel' is part 'spiritual atmosphere', part 'fineness of the language'; together, these qualities 'define' the nation, or Englishness. The strangeness of Gard's position becomes more evident when we consider the writers he implies are possibly less definitive of England than Austen: Shakespeare, Eliot, and Dickens. All three writers openly embrace within their writing historical perspectives on the making of England; they are panoramic writers who strove towards what was, in their own terms, inclusiveness. Nevertheless, through the magic of paradox, the provincial and marginal Austen is somehow more central.

Somebody once commented that Poland was not a country but a state of mind. England, conversely, is not a state, let alone a state of mind, so much as it is country, landscape, patchworks of fields with sportive hedgerows run wild, village greens, pubs, a big house and tithed cottages. 'England' is, or was, a Home Counties topography, hence the special agony of the rural south in the foot-and-mouth epidemic of 2001, with the threat it posed to 'our way of life', and the bemused indifference of the urban masses. As that branch of the heritage industry known as the BBC drama department informs us – although we could go to Hollywood to find the same message – Austen is the genius of this topography. So another paradoxical aspect of Austen's status as England's special thing is that she actually spends very little time directly describing England's green and pleasant land. Whatever else Austen is, she is not its poet. She is, rather, a poet of domestic spaces.

As we have seen, critics make much of the way Austen's novels are inflected by the landscaping debates that were so central to the political self-consciousness of the late eighteenth century. Landscaping was not about private space. As the landscape gardens at Stowe especially make evident, they were understood as the means of intervening within the public sphere. Like the Gardiners visiting Pemblerly in *Pride and Prejudice*, the aspiring as well as the established classes visited the grand country houses and their grounds, which were to be 'read'. Visiting Stowe was itself a cultural institution, one served by a small library of maps and guidebooks designed to help the visitor to read the political iconography of the gardens and temples. The proliferating media may have made the garden-as-political-pamphlet redundant by the end of the eighteenth century, but the habit of reading the landscape politically, as a locus of Englishness, remained. William Gilpin, Uvedale Price, Richard Payne Knight, and Humphry Repton may have been part of a movement that aestheticized land-scaping (Gilpin's *Dialogues on the Garden at Stowe* is a particu-larly informative document in this respect), but landscaping still contained a political charge, not least because of the issues raised by such large-scale interventions, in which entire villages were relocated, as in Capability Brown's refashioning of the landscape around Chatsworth in Derbyshire. The conspicuous involvement of Whig grandees in the reshaping of the countryside, such as Lord Cobham and the Duke of Devonshire, was also relevant. Moreover, in the Revolutionary times in which Austen wrote, 'change' of any sort could not remain uncontaminated by the debates that raged for, or against, innovation. What was at stake was at once the fabric of the constitution, and the fabric of the nation, which inevitably include its physical appearance, its landscape.

Landscaping on a grand and therefore political scale is a prominent feature of *Northanger Abbey* and *Mansfield Park*, and critics have taken advantage of Austen's apparent engagement with this politicized debate to pin down her own position, whether she is pro- or anti-improvement.[26] In my reading of her, Austen is not just anti-improvement, she is anti-landscap-ing, *tout court*. Her position, as I read it, is virtually Burkean. If she is motivated by 'landscape', it is to satirize it as a misbegotten project, whatever the degree of 'improvement' or the sensitivity of the improver. Her positive depictions of landscape, her own excursions into representing England's green and pleasant land, are remarkably few. The passage in *Persuasion*, where she lets herself go, and, in an apparent surrender to the Romantic Zeitgeist, describes the picturesque verdure winding its way up a cliff outside Lyme Regis, scarcely comes to half a page (*P*. 86). More typical of Austen is this description from *Emma*, where Mr Knightly escorts his guests around the grounds of Donwell Abbey:

> It was hot; and after walking some time over the gardens in a scattered, dispersed way, scarcely any three together, they insensibly followed one another to the delicious shade of a broad short avenue of limes, which stretching beyond the garden at an equal distance from the river, seemed the finish of the pleasure grounds. – It led to nothing; nothing but a view at the end over a low stone wall with high pillars, which seemed intended, in their erection, to give the appearance of an approach to the house, which never had been there. Disputable, however, as might be the taste of such a termination, it was itself a charming walk, and the view which closed it extremely pretty. – The considerable slope, at nearly the foot of which the Abbey stood, gradually acquired a steeper form beyond its grounds; and at half a mile distant was a bank of considerable abruptness and grandeur, well clothed with wood; – and at the bottom of this bank, favourably placed and sheltered, rose the Abbey-Mill farm, with meadows in front, and the river making a close and handsome curve around it. (*E*. 297)

One of the significant aspects of this passage is that it does not represent Emma's point of view. It seems to be Austen herself speaking, albeit in her customary fashion of satiric indirection. When the narrator says 'it led to nothing', she mimics, for a moment, the voice of a landscape connoisseur, for whom, indeed, the scene would hold nothing. There is no ha-ha, nor for that matter a gate to frame the view beyond, and thus render it picturesque. There is, however, a semblance of such a thing, in the twin pillars. This feature has not been designed or 'improved', but by a happy accident – by nature or instinct – it works as 'an appearance of an approach to the house'. When the narrator disputes its tastefulness, she once again teases us with her insincerity, as she clearly does believe in its tastefulness, but it is the tastefulness of time and tide, and not of conscious choice or fashionable affectation. It is also on a domestic, rather than a grand, scale: it is 'charming' and 'pretty'. Donwell Abbey is placed, not for show, but for comfort; and it is echoed across the way by Abbey Mill Farm, the home of the estate's tenant farmer, Robert Martin. It is physically 'sheltered', but also metaphorically so, for Robert Martin enjoys the protection of Mr Knightley's patronage and enlightened advocacy: the scene figures the ideal landowner and his appreciative tenant. This is a landscape, not of objects, of physical features arranged picturesquely, but of social relation. It is, as I earlier argued, a Burkean, or Tory, pastoral. Borrowing a phrase from *Northanger Abbey* describing Woodston parsonage, itself echoing Uvedale Price, Donwell Abbey is what Marilyn Butler calls a 'well-connected' landscape.[27]

The narrator then breaks cover to pronounce upon it: 'It was a sweet view – sweet to the eye and the mind. English verdure, English culture, English comfort, seen under a sun bright, without being oppressive.' In itself, the passage enacts the 'nondiscursive kernel of enjoyment' that lends 'England' its 'ontological consistency'. The passage is a series of qualifications, each one taking us through another layer as we approach nearer the 'kernel'. 'Sweet', like 'domestic', informs us that we are within an English (but of course also a pastoral) *via media* that is silently set against its ever-present other: French ostentation, or overbearing, despotic grandeur, a qualification that also 'others' England's un-English aristocracy, with its flair for grandiose gardens. The first qualification puts aside any possible confusion with these palaces of sensuality, for the view was sweet, not to the taste, or senses, but to the 'eye and the mind', with the one the portal of the other. 'English verdure' loses any purely botanical significance (meaning flora peculiar to England) with each succeeding qualification: the verdure is English by dint of cultivation or culture, not nature; and it produces comfort (in the dual sense of ease and prosperity) rather than mere pleasure. England as a happy *via media* is clinched in the last sentence: the sun is bright, but not oppressive; English, but not French.

We appear to have arrived at an explanation for why Austen's has become England's 'our thing': she articulates, not a topography of the soul, a green and pleasant land through which one might wander, or take one's leisure, but a series of social relations: a series of relations as English to Englishmen, in the national mythology, as roast beef: an England of harmonious ranks who might be found, at once, *en masse*, as a testament to the organic bonds that tie, playing cricket on the village green. As the myth had it, the nation that played cricket together, stayed together, a myth once again in stark contrast to France, where non-cricketing squires came unstuck, not just from the community, but from their bodies.

This is, however, a delusive explanation, at least as far as it stands. The simple fact is, this was not how Austen was received. She was not immediately acclaimed as an English writer, a writer of peculiar Englishness. She was barely acclaimed at all; as Clifford Siskin has pointed out, according to her contemporary critics, her main virtue was inoffensiveness.[28] Up until her nephew's biography, in 1870, she was understood to be a minority interest.[29] And, while there was a view that she was, as a novelist, *sui generis*, her rarity was not nationalistically inflected. Or, if she was marked as English, it was done from outside, by American writers expressing their contempt for the narrowness of her writing, such as Ezra Pound expostulating against the 'dull, stupid, hemmed-in sort of life' of her novels, or others affirming their Anglophilia through praise for the self-same qualities.[30] James Edward Austen-Leigh's biography did not beget Austen mania; an upsurge of interest in Austen was already afoot. Nevertheless it remains the case that Austen was acclaimed as a peculiarly English writer long after the fact; and this must be our starting point for understanding Austen as England's special thing.

Brian Southam contrasts the growing Janeite phenomenon in England with something similar happening in America: 'Her admirers began to regard the world of the novels as a version of Home Counties existence, of gracious living, of "courtesy and breeding", to quote Lady Mary Sackville's Introduction to a book of *Selections* in 1913.'[31] My hypothesis, then, is this: Austen relates to English nationalism in the same way that Macpherson does to Scots nationalism, or the revival of the Bardic tradition does to the Welsh. In other words, Austen is a sign for the English (for some English) of the connection and continuity between the primitive past and the sophisticated present. As the dominant country, England did not need the kind of national genealogies required by subject 'nations', such as the Welsh, Scots, or Irish – that is to say, genealogies underwriting a wished-for ethnic and political congruity. What was required, rather, was a commodity that validated England's contemporary *telos*, its version of the good life, which was, of course, a version of pastoral. Austen's novels filled that role. They did not fill that role at the time when they were written. On the contrary, the contemporary inflections of Austen's novels key us into the difficulties of England's transition from a pre-growth to a growth economy. But by the early years of the twentieth century, the victory of the growth economy was complete, and the pains of the transition registered by Austen were either forgotten or embalmed as nostalgia. It was thus both possible, and desirable, to recast Austen as an unproblematic signifier of the 'good life' embedded within a Home Counties ideology.

I earlier referred to the theory of 'gentlemanly capitalism' advanced by the economic historians P. J. Cain and A. G. Hopkins. By this phrase they mean the predominance of the City of London in Britain's economic life, where wealth is generated through the 'genteel' means of financial instruments rather than through industrial development. Unlike America or Germany, Britain never went through 'Fordism' (other than through the extension of Ford, or investment from overseas). In comparison with its international competitors, Britain did not invest substantially in mass production. The City's preferred means of earning money was to invest capital in financially sound dominions or client states that would repay the loans through the exploitation of the dominion's natural resources. Britain's foreign policy was thus aimed, not at the preservation of British colonies abroad, but at the preservation of sound financial regimes that could be counted upon not to renege on the debts necessarily contracted through the City. Cain and Hopkins would argue that the legacy of gentlemanly capitalism is still with us. The crucial point, though, is that the apogee of gentlemanly capitalism corresponds with the period in which Austen was first recast as England's special thing.

In the hundred or so years following on from Austen's death, it might have seemed to be the case that industrialization was altering the balance of power between North and South. Industrialization led to population growth in the north, as well as to new sources of wealth. But the country's financial centre of gravity has always been the south-east, a state of affairs that has become more pronounced in recent years. England's version of pastoral is a Home Counties version, because that is the political, financial, and ideological centre of England. If the material reality of its wealth is the City, the ideological illusion it underpins is that its financial beneficiaries are nationalist 'primitives', indigenous folk living out the ageless rituals of the countryside, with their age-old Range Rovers, Agas, and farmhouse kitchens – and, of course, Jane Austen.

Once we see Austen as England's totem of primitive Englishness (where all I mean by 'primitive' is the mythic aura of origins), a great deal of Austen's reception falls neatly into place. For instance, Southam shows that, against the evidence of the memoir, and against the grain of the early nineteenth-century criticism, Austen was constructed in the 1870s and 1880s as a natural songbird.[32] This was not only how she was constructed: it was how she was marketed. It is a conjunction that had happened once before, in the consummation of eighteenth-century bardolatry. Shakespeare, too, was constructed as a figure of natural genius and marketed as a commodity through the deluxe editions of Boydell and others. He was also an ideological figure for English nationalism. Austen's canonization, as national literary saint, coincides with her being turned into a commodity; she is nationalized, as Shakespeare was, and, like Shakespeare, she has to be constructed as artless, as the natural expression of primitive Englishness – where 'primitive' has the oxymoronic character of natural genius. One might argue that the apogee of the marketing of Austen as a nationalist fetish was the ten-volume Dent edition of 1892:

> Headed by the charming (and unauthentic) 'Zoffany' portrait, illustrated by William Cooke, and with ornaments by F. C. Tilney, it was an item for the fastidious book-lover and offered such decorative features as a two-colour title-page, top edges gilt, and Ex Libris panels. The bindings carry elaborate gold die-stamping. The title of the novel is presented within a regal cartouche, topped with the Austen family crest (a stag rampant). If this is the touch

147

aristocratic, the touch personal is added by the signature 'J. Austen' in facsimile, bottom right, also in gold. The illustrations, printed in a rich dark sepia, on parchmenty paper, are individually leaved with protective tissue. The hint of preciousness in all this decorative elaboration is heightened by the diminutive size of the volumes. The pages are only 4¼ by 6¾ inches, giving the whole an effect, as it might be described, of tasteful daintiness. To this is added a confusing dash of the quaintly antique in gothic black-letter chapter-heads, the numerals so mannered as to remain indecipherable. If all this offends the purist bibliophile, it is a confection which displays a vigorous (if broadsided) marketing instinct.[33]

One might especially wonder about the Gothic lettering, given that few writers are so obviously un-Gothic as Jane Austen, as she herself made manifest in *Northanger Abbey*. We might wonder, that is, until we recall that, for Britain's nineteenth-century cultural elite, Gothic was the English style, witness (and one need go no further than this) the renovated Houses of Parliament.[34]

CONCLUSION

Why is Austen the best loved of English authors? Because her unprecedented ability to create the illusion of personality within the novel form speaks so strongly to our Romantic individualism and to our condition as readers caught up in the contradictions of what Deidre Lynch calls 'reading in a crowd'. Why is she perceived as being peculiarly English? Because her Tory pastorals fit seamlessly into the mythic needs of modern English nationalism. However, it is also clear that there is an unceasing appetite among non-English readers for England's special 'thing', which we might think contradictory. The American T. B. Shaw, writing in 1849, offers us insight into why this is not so: 'Whoever desires to know the interior life of that vast and admirable body the rural gentry of England – a body which absolutely exists in no other country on earth, and to which the nation owes many of its most valuable characteristics – must read the novels of Jane Austen.'[35] Shaw writes from the perspective of an American modernity – of a social scene lamented by writers such as Nathaniel

Hawthorne and Henry James as lacking in England's richly textured communities – in which England's teeming gentry are the backbone of the nation. Globalization has only accentuated this nostalgic apprehension of England's stalwart, anachronistic nature, as a kind of bastion against an all-vanquishing, homogenizing modernity. In Shaw's apprehension of England, there is no mention, or rather no sense of, the abundant rural poor, let alone the huddled masses congregating in England's northern, industrializing cities. If for the English reader Austen is the talismanic presence that authenticates a Home Counties genealogy of what it means to be English (which is why, it has to be remembered, many English readers have difficulty with her), for the non-English reader Austen is, one suspects, something like the reverse: evidence that England's 'gentry' endure still as the repository of England's most valuable characteristics, a token that there exists, somewhere, a precious cultural redoubt withstanding globalization's irresistible tide. In such circumstances, the Jane Austen experience is a fairly necessary adjunct to the modern lifestyle. Until, of course, we look closely into the writing and discover it is not so simple.

Notes

INTRODUCTION

1. Quoted in Roger Gard, *Jane Austen's Novels: The Art of Clarity* (Cambridge, Mass.: Harvard University Press, 1994), 14.
2. Ibid. 12.
3. For a history of the Janeites, see Claudia L. Johnson, 'Austen Cults and Cultures', in Edward Copeland and Juliet McMaster (eds.), *The Cambridge Companion to Jane Austen* (Cambridge: Cambridge University Press, 1997), 211–26. Cf. Deirdre Lynch (ed.), *Janeites: Austen's Disciples and Devotees* (Princeton: Princeton University Press, 2000).
4. For a discussion of Austen's perceived Englishness and her absorption into the heritage industry, see Roger Sales, *Jane Austen and Representations of Regency England* (London: Routledge, 1994), 3–27.
5. Brian Southam (ed.), *Jane Austen: The Critical Heritage*, 2 vols. (London: Routledge & Kegan Paul, 1987), ii, 17–19.
6. D. W. Harding, 'Regulated Hatred', in Harding, *Regulated Hatred and Other Essays on Jane Austen*, ed. Monica Lawlor (London: Athlone Press, 1998). Harding's essay was originally published in 1940.
7. Marvin Murdrick, *Jane Austen: Irony as Defense and Discovery* (Berkeley and Los Angeles: University of California Press, 1952); John Halperin, *The Life of Jane Austen* (Baltimore: Johns Hopkins University Press, 1996).
8. Lionel Trilling, 'Why we Read Jane Austen', in Trilling, *The Last Decade: Essays and Reviews, 1965–75*, ed. Diana Trilling (Oxford: Oxford University Press, 1982), 204–25.
9. Edward Said, *Culture and Imperialism* (London: Chatto & Windus, 1993).
10. Terry Castle, 'Sister, Sister', review of *Jane Austen's Letters*, ed. Deirdre Le Faye, *London Review of Books*, 3 Aug. 1995.
11. Halperin, *The Life of Jane Austen*, p. ix.

12. D.A. Miller, 'Austen's Attitude', *Yale Journal of Criticism: Interpretation in the Humanities*, 8 (1995), 1–5.
13. Marilyn Butler, *Jane Austen and the War of Ideas* (1974; repr. Oxford: Clarendon Press, 1987).
14. For a counterview of Austen as a Romantic, rather than anti-Romantic writer, see Clifford Siskin, 'A Formal Development: Austen, the Novel, and Romanticism', *Centennial Review*, 29 (1985), 1–28; for recent debate on Austen's feminism, see Devoney Looser (ed.), *Jane Austen and Discourses of Feminism* (New York: St Martin's Press, 1995); for Austen as an emergent feminist, see Claudia L. Johnson, *Jane Austen: Women, Politics and the Novel* (Chicago: University of Chicago Press, 1988).
15. For examples, see Juliet McMaster and Bruce Stovel (eds.), *Jane Austen's Business: Her World and her Profession* (Basingstoke: Macmillan, 1996); Edward Copeland, *Women Writing about Money: Women's Fiction in England, 1790–1820* (Cambridge: Cambridge University Press, 1995); and Johnson, *Jane Austen*.
16. For a discussion of the theoretical difficulties involved in pinning down Austen's affiliations, see Isobel Armstrong, ' "Conservative" Jane Austen? – Some Views', in Armstrong, *Mansfield Park*, Penguin Critical Studies (Harmondsworth: Penguin, 1988), 94–104.
17. Harold Bloom, *Shakespeare: The Invention of the Human* (London: Fourth Estate, 1999).
18. Southam (ed.), *Jane Austen: The Critical Heritage*, ii. 15. For a history of critics comparing Austen with Shakespeare, see ii. 20–1.
19. This distinction is a simplified version of the one drawn by Brean S. Hammond, 'The Political Unconscious in *Mansfield Park*', in Nigel Wood (ed.), *Mansfield Park* (Buckingham: Open University Press, 1993), 56–87.

CHAPTER 1. PERSONALITY IN AUSTEN

1. The point is also made by Deidre Lynch, *The Economy of Character: Novels, Market Culture, and the Business of Inner Meaning* (Chicago: University of Chicago Press, 1998), 1. For a more traditional approach, see John Bayley, *The Characters of Love: A Study of the Literature of Personality* (London: Constable, 1960).
2. Richard Simpson, unsigned review of James Edward Austen-Leigh, *A Memoir of Jane Austen* (1870), *North British Review*, 52 (Apr. 1870), 129–52, in Brian Southam (ed.), *Jane Austen: The Critical Heritage*, 2 vols. (London: Routledge & Kegan Paul, 1968), i, 250.

3. Barbara Hardy, Introduction, in George Eliot, *Daniel Deronda* (Harmondsworth: Penguin, 1977), 19.

4. Henri Bergson, *Laughter: An Essay on the Meaning of the Comic*, trans. Cloudesley Brereton (London: Macmillan, 1921).

5. E. M. Forster, *Aspects of the Novel* (London: E. Arnold, 1949).

6. Gary Kelly, 'Religion and Politics', in Edward Copeland and Juliet McMaster (eds.), *The Cambridge Companion to Jane Austen* (Cambridge: Cambridge University Press, 1997), 149–69.

7. For an extended treatment of the relationship between Austen's novel and the politics of the 1790s, see Ros Ballaster, Introduction, in *Sense and Sensibility* (Harmondsworth: Penguin, 1995).

8. Chris Jones, *Radical Sensibility* (London: Routledge, 1993).

9. Pitt introduced a tax on hair powder to help fund the war against France. Wearing one's hair naturally, without powder, was understood as a political gesture in the 1790s.

10. E. J. Clery and Robert Miles (eds.), *Gothic Documents: A Sourcebook, 1700–1820* (Manchester: Manchester University Press, 2000), 237–8.

11. Richard Whateley, unsigned review of *Northanger Abbey* and *Persuasion*, *Quarterly Review*, 24 (Jan. 1821), 352–76, repr. in Southam (ed.), *Jane Austen: The Critical Heritage*, i. 95.

12. Ibid. 87. Whateley is in fact quoting Walter Scott's review of *Emma*, which had also appeared in the *Quarterly Review*; see Southam (ed.), *Jane Austen: The Critical Heritage*, i. 59.

13. To J. Edward Austen, 16 Dec. 1816, *Jane Austen's Letters to her Sister Cassandra and Others*, ed. R .W. Chapman, 2nd edn. (Oxford: Oxford University Press, 1952), 469.

14. W. D. Howells, quoted in Brian Southam (ed.), *Jane Austen: The Critical Heritage, 1870–1940*, 2 vols. (London: Routledge & Kegan Paul, 1987), ii, 29.

15. Whateley, repr. in Southam (ed.), *Jane Austen: The Critical Heritage*, i. 88.

16. For example, compare with William Godwin's 1797 essay, 'On History and Romance', in Clery and Miles (eds.), *Gothic Documents*, 260–5, which also argues that the romance, or novel, is more philosophical than history. See also Marilyn Butler, Introduction, in *Northanger Abbey* (Harmondsworth: Penguin, 1995), p. xviii.

17. Richard Rorty, 'Comments on Castoriadis's "The End of Philosophy"', *Salmagundi*, 82–3 (1989), 24–30.

18. Lionel Trilling, 'Manners, Morals, and the Novel', in Trilling, *The Liberal Imagination: Essays on Literature and Society* (London: Secker & Warburg, 1951), 216.

19. Lionel Trilling, 'Art and Fortune', in Trilling, *The Liberal Imagination*, 260.

20. Juliet McMaster, 'Class', in Copeland and McMaster (eds.), *Cambridge Companion*, 117.

21. For a discussion, see Marilyn Butler, *Jane Austen and the War of Ideas* (1974; repr. Oxford: Clarendon Press, 1987); Claudia L. Johnson, *Jane Austen: Women, Politics and the Novel* (Chicago: University Press of Chicago, 1988). For a general background, see Janet Todd, *Sensibility: An Introduction* (London: Methuen, 1986).

22. Alistair M. Duckworth, *The Improvement of the Estate: A Study of Jane Austen's Novels* (Baltimore: Johns Hopkins University Press, 1994).

23. Chris Jones, *Radical Sensibility* (London: Routledge, 1993).

24. For example, in a letter to her sister Cassandra (11 Oct. 1813) Austen agrees that Mary Brunton's *Self-Control* is 'an excellently-meant, elegantly-written Work', but is 'without anything of Nature or Probability . . . I declare I do not know whether Laura's passage down the American river, is not the most natural, possible, everyday thing she ever does' (*Jane Austen's Letters*, ed. Chapman, 345).

25. Miriam Allott, *Novelists on the Novel* (London: Routledge & Kegan Paul, 1959). See especially the first two sections, 'The Novel and the Marvellous' and 'The Novel as a Portrait of Life', 41–82.

26. Quoted in David Monaghan, '*Mansfield Park* and Evangelicism: A Reassessment', in Ian Littlewood (ed.), *Jane Austen: Critical Assessments*, 4 vols. (Mountfield: Helm Information, 1998), iv. 173. The passage from Burke is from *Letters on a Regicide Peace*.

27. Richard Poirier, *A World Elsewhere: The Place of Style in American Literature* (Oxford: Oxford University Press, 1966).

CHAPTER 2. GENRE

1. Deidre Lynch, *The Economy of Character: Novels, Market Culture, and the Business of Inner Meaning* (Chicago: University of Chicago Press, 1998), 4.

2. *The Journal of Sir Walter Scott*, ed. David Douglas, 2 vols. (Edinburgh, 1890), i. 155.

3. The claim has often been made by critics arguing the case for the difference of American romance. For example, see Lionel Trilling, 'Manners, Morals, and the Novel' and 'Art and Fortune', in Trilling, *The Liberal Imagination: Essays on Literature and Society* (London: Secker & Warburg, 1951), 205–22, 255–80; Marius Bewley, *The Eccentric Design: Form in the Classic American Novel* (New York: Columbia University Press, 1959); Richard Poirier, *A*

World Elsewhere: The Place of Style in American Literature (Oxford: Oxford University Press, 1966); A. N. Kaul, *The American Vision: Actual and Ideal Society in Nineteenth-Century Fiction* (New Haven: Yale University Press, 1963).

4. See James Grossman, *James Fenimore Cooper* (London: Methuen & Co., 1950), 17. There is some uncertainty whether the English novel that spurred Cooper's first novel, *Precaution*, was Austen's.

5. Brian Southam (ed.), *Jane Austin: The Critical Heritage, 1870–1940*, 2 vols. (London: Routledge & Kegan Paul, 1987), ii, 232.

6. Isobel Armstrong, ' "Conservative" Jane Austen? – Some Views', in Stephen Regan (ed.), *The Nineteenth-Century Novel: A Critical Reader* (London: Routledge, 2001), 170.

7. See Peter Garside, 'The English Novel in the Romantic Era: Consolidation and Dispersal', in Peter Garside and Rainer Schöwerling (eds.), *The English Novel 1770–1829: A Bibliographical Survey of Prose Fiction Published in the British Isles*, ii. *1800–1829* (General Editors: Peter Garside, James Raven, and Rainer Schöwerling; Oxford: Oxford University Press, 2000), 50, 56.

8. Charles R. Maturin, *Women; or, Pour et contre* (Edinburgh: Archibald Constable, 1818), p. iv.

9. Garside, 'The English Novel', 74.

10. *Jane Austen's Letters to her Sister Cassandra and Others*, ed. R. W. Chapman, 2nd edn. (Oxford: Oxford University Press, 1952), 452.

11. For a discussion and references, see Robert Miles, *Gothic Writing 1750–1820: A Genealogy*, 2nd edn. (Manchester: Manchester University Press, 2002), 135–6.

12. Northrop Frye, *Anatomy of Criticism: Four Essays* (Princeton: Princeton University Press, 1971), 163.

13. William Empson, 'Hamlet when New', *Sewanee Review*, 61 (1953), 15–42, 185–205.

14. Austen's horror of cliché is nicely illustrated in a passage from a letter to her niece offering her advice on novel writing: 'Devereux Forester's being ruined by his vanity is extremely good; but I wish you would not let him plunge into a "vortex of Dissipation". I do not object to the Thing, but I cannot bear the expression; it is such thorough novel slang – and so old, that I dare say Adam met with it in the first novel he opened . . .' (to Anna Austen, 28 Sept. 1814, *Jane Austen's Letters*, ed. Chapman, 404).

15. For an ethnographic approach to Austen's representation of Georgian kinship practices, see Richard Handler and Daniel Segal, *Jane Austen and the Fiction of Culture: An Essay on the Narration of Social Realities*, 2nd edn. (Lanham, Md.: Rowman & Littlefield, 1999).

16. For an extended treatment of this aspect of Rousseau, see Miles, *Gothic Writing*, 78–82.
17. Michel Foucault, *The History of Sexuality*, i. *An Introduction*, trans. Robert Hurley (Harmondsworth: Penguin, 1979).
18. Gary Kelly, 'Religion and Politics', in Edward Copeland and Juliet McMaster (eds.), *The Cambridge Companion to Jane Austen* (Cambridge: Cambridge University Press, 1997), 149–69.
19. For evidence of Austen's sensitivity to this issue, see Ros Ballaster's comments on Austen's revisions to *Sense and Sensibility* (*Sense and Sensibility*, ed. Ros Ballaster (Harmondsworth: Penguin, 1995), 327.
20. Aristotle, 'On the Art of Poetry', in *Aristotle/Horace/Longinus: Classical Literary Criticism*, trans. T. S. Dorsch (Harmondsworth: Penguin, 1965), 46.
21. P. J. Cain and A. G. Hopkins, *British Imperialism: Innovation and Expansion, 1688–1914* (London: Longman, 1993).
22. To Cassandra, 21 Apr. 1805, *Jane Austen's Letters*, ed. Chapman, 155.
23. Marilyn Butler makes a similar point about Austen's 'proto-anthropological technique' of anatomizing a society through the matching of characters and their possessions: 'In *Emma*, Harriet's stub of pencil and Mr Woodhouse's smooth, thin water-gruel speak volumes about their two possessors . . .' (Butler, Introduction, in *Northanger Abbey* (Harmondsworth: Penguin, 1995), p. xxiv).
24. For two useful introductions to the pastoral, see Peter Marinelli, *The Pastoral* (London: Methuen, 1971), and William Empson, *Some Versions of Pastoral* (London: Chatto & Windus, 1950).
25. For 1790s radical politics, see Iain McCalman, *Radical Underworld: Prophets, Revolutionaries, and Pornographers in London* (Oxford: Clarendon Press, 1993); John Barrell, *Imagining the King's Death: Figurative Treason, Fantasies of Regicide, 1793–1796* (Oxford: Oxford University Press, 2000); for Austen and politics, see Claudia L. Johnson, *Jane Austen: Women, Politics and the Novel* (Chicago: University of Chicago Press, 1988); Warren Roberts, *Jane Austen and the French Revolution* (London: Athlone Press, 1995); and Mary Evans, *Jane Austen and the State* (London: Tavistock Publications, 1987).
26. See e.g. Marilyn Butler (ed.), *Burke, Paine, Godwin and the Revolution Controversy* (Cambridge: Cambridge University Press, 1984); Roger Sales, *Jane Austen and Representations of Regency England* (London: Routledge, 1994).
27. Sales, *Jane Austen*, 169.

28. In 1751 the Bank of England offered consolidated stock at 3 per cent, a rate of return that remained unchanged until the nineteenth century. The phrase the 'three per cents' signalled those whose capital was invested in this way. As Edward Copeland points out, and, as Austen repeatedly tells us, owing to the war, the going rate of return during this period was 5 per cent (Copeland, 'Money', in Copeland and McMaster (eds.), *The Cambridge Companion*, 134).

29. Anon., review of *Emma*, in the *Champion*, 31 Mar. 1816, 102–3; repr. *Nineteenth-Century Fiction*, 26/4 (Mar. 1972), 469–74.

30. Q. D. Leavis, 'Jane Austen: Novelist of a Changing Society', in Leavis, *Collected Essays*, i. *The Englishness of the English Novel*, ed. G. Singh (Cambridge: Cambridge University Press, 1983), 26–60. Leavis notes how the Great House is in a state of transition and 'improvement', a cross between the modern, informal style of Uppercross cottage and old-fashioned Kellynch (50–1).

31. Richard Cronin, private correspondence.

32. John Halperin, *The Life of Jane Austen* (Baltimore: Johns Hopkins University Press, 1996), 125.

CHAPTER 3. POINT OF VIEW

1. On receiving proofs for *Pride and Prejudice*, Austen remarks that 'a "said he", or a "said she", would sometimes make the dialogue more immediately clear; but

   > I do not write for such dull elves
   > As have not a great deal of ingenuity themselves.'

   (To Cassandra, 29 Jan. 1813, *Jane Austen's Letters to her Sister Cassandra and Others*, ed. R. W. Chapman, 2nd edn. (Oxford: Oxford University Press, 1952), 298.)

2. Chris Jones, ' "Nothing that did not Answer": Jane Austen and Romantic Interrogation', paper delivered at Sustaining Romanticism, Seventh International BARS Conference, Liverpool, July 2001.

3. Quoted in Peter Monaghan, 'Sex and Sensibility, Scholars Redefine Jane Austen', *Chronicle of Higher Education*, 17 Aug. 2001.

4. Marilyn Butler, 'Introduction', in *Northanger Abbey* (Harmondsworth: Penguin, 1995), pp. xxi–xxx.

5. Deidre Lynch, *The Economy of Character: Novels, Market Culture, and the Business of Inner Meaning* (Chicago: University of Chicago Press, 1998).

6. For introductory works on free indirect speech, see Roy Pascal, *The Dual Voice: Free Indirect Speech and its Functioning in the Nineteenth-Century European Novel* (Manchester: Manchester University Press, 1977); Ronald Carter (ed.), *Language and Literature: An Introductory Reader in Stylistics* (London: Routledge, 1991); Katie Wales, *A Dictionary of Stylistics*, 2nd edn. (Harlow: Pearson Education, 2001).

7. As argued by Marilyn Butler, 'Introduction', pp. xii–xiv.

8. There is a kind of exception to this in her later works, such as *Emma*, where Austen represents her heroine in discussion with herself, and here she does use quotation marks (for an example, see *E*. 155).

9. On the unlikelihood of Austen revising her novel after 1803, see Butler, 'Introduction', p. xiii.

10. See above, Ch. 2 n. 10.

11. Butler, 'Introduction', pp. xiv–xxi.

12. For example, see Mary Wollstonecraft, *The Vindications: 'The Rights of Men' and 'The Rights of Woman'*, ed. D. L. Macdonald and Kathleen Scherf (Peterborough, Ontario: Broadview Press, 1997), 215.

13. See above, Ch. 1 n. 15.

14. Lionel Trilling, 'Art and Fortune', in Trilling, *The Liberal Imagination: Essays on Literature and Society* (London: Secker & Warburg, 1951), 260.

15. Jerome McGann, *The Poetics of Sensibility: A Revolution in Literary Style* (Oxford: Clarendon Press, 1996), 6.

16. David Monaghan, '*Mansfield Park* and Evangelicanism: A Reassessment', in Ian Littlewood (ed.), *Jane Austen: Critical Assessments*, 4 vols. (Mountfield: Helm Information, 1998), iv. 167–79.

17. Anthony Mandal, 'Jane Austen and the Production of Fiction, 1785–1818', unpublished Ph.D. thesis (University of Wales, 2001), 162–9.

18. Ibid. 148–9.

19. Mary Poovey, *The Proper Lady and the Woman Writer: Ideology as Style in the Works of Mary Wollstonecraft, Mary Shelley, and Jane Austen* (Chicago: University of Chicago Press, 1984).

20. See above, Ch. 1 n. 24.

21. Mandal, 'Jane Austen and the Production of Fiction, 1785–1818', 192–4.

22. Monaghan goes further and argues that, in siding with conduct against conversion, Burke against Wilberforce, Austen actively criticizes the evangelicals whom she associates with the metropolitan society then threatening the country way of life: '*Mansfield*

Park is a novel written in defense of a beleaguered society and its religion; the Evangelicals were part of the forces of change. As such, they can have had no appeal for Jane Austen' (Monaghan, '*Mansfield Park* and Evangelicanism'), iv. 177.

23. Lionel Trilling, '*Mansfield Park*', in Claudia L. Johnson (ed.), *Mansfield Park: A Norton Critical Edition* (New York: W. W. Norton & Co., 1997), 431.

24. Edward Said, *Culture and Imperialism* (London: Chatto & Windus, 1993).

25. Brian Southam, 'The Silence of the Bertrams', in Johnson (ed.), *Mansfield Park: A Norton Critical Edition*, 493–8.

26. 'There is something distinctly "modern-built", *nouveau* and West Indian about Sir Thomas and his social standing, a point worth making as some commentators wholly misplace Sir Thomas, writing about him as a member of the old and established landed gentry . . .' (ibid. 497).

27. See Joseph Lew, ' "That Abominable Traffic": *Mansfield Park* and the Dynamics of Slavery', in Johnson (ed.), *Mansfield Park: A Norton Critical Edition*, 498–510.

CHAPTER 4. NATIONALISM, GENDER, CLASS

1. Quoted in Brian Southam (ed.), *Jane Austen: The Critical Heritage, 1870–1940*, 2 vols. (London: Routledge & Kegan Paul, 1987), ii, 87–8.

2. For Austen's scandalous relatives, see David Nokes, *Jane Austen: A Life* (London: Fourth Estate, 1997); for the remaining references, see above, Introduction.

3. John Sekora, *Luxury: The Concept in Western Thought, Eden to Smollett* (Baltimore: Johns Hopkins University Press, 1977).

4. Ernest Gellner, *Nations and Nationalism* (Oxford: Blackwell, 1983), and *Nationalism* (London: Phoenix, 1998). Other standard references include E. J. Hobsbawm, *Nations and Nationalism since 1780: Programme, Myth and Reality* (Cambridge: Cambridge University Press, 1990) and Benedict Anderson, whose *Imagined Communities* (London: Verso, 1983) advances a similar view to Gellner's, in which nationalism is linked to the development of print culture.

5. Gellner, *Nations*, 1.

6. Gellner, *Nationalism*, 17.

7. Ibid. 34.

8. Gellner, *Nations*, 1.

9. Quoted by Linda Colley, *Britons: Forging the Nation 1707–1837* (New Haven: Yale University Press, 1992), 20.

10. Hobsbawm, *Nations and Nationalism*, 90.
11. Gellner, *Nations*, 125.
12. Hobsbawm, *Nations and Nationalism*, 84.
13. Lionel Trilling, 'Why we Read Jane Austen', in Trilling, *The Last Decade: Essays and Reviews, 1965–75*, ed. Diana Trilling (Oxford: Oxford University Press, 1982), 204–25.
14. Southam (ed.), *Jane Austen: The Critical Heritage*, ii. 77.
15. Quoted in John Halperin, *The Life of Jane Austen* (Baltimore: Johns Hopkins University Press, 1996), 59.
16. Brean Hammond makes the point that Henry Crawford is rendered effeminate through his aesthetic interests in landscaping and acting – in luxury and 'personality' – in contrast with William Price's masculine militarism: that William does, while Crawford 'speculates' ('The Political Unconscious in *Mansfield Park*', in Nigel Wood (ed.), *Mansfield Park* (Buckingham: Open University Press, 1993), 56–87.
17. The following comment by Scott is typical: 'There is a truth of painting in her writings which always delights me. They do not, it is true, get above the middle classes of society, but there she is inimitable' (*The Journal of Sir Walter Scott*, ed. David Douglas, 2 vols. (Edinburgh, 1890), ii. 37). See Southam (ed.), *Jane Austen: The Critical Heritage*, i, for more examples.
18. Chatsworth is mentioned as being on the Gardiner's itinerary, so Pemberley cannot be a pseudonym for Chatsworth; but it is spoken of as being one of the principal houses of Derbyshire, which is what Chatsworth is.
19. Lionel Trilling, 'Manners, Morals, and the Novel', in Trilling, *The Liberal Imagination: Essays on Literature and Society* (London: Secker & Warburg, 1951), 205–22.
20. The full reference for Sir Walter's favourite reading is John Debrett, *The Baronetage of England; containing their descent and present state; their collateral branches, births, marriages and issues, from the institution of the order, in 1611; a complete and alphabetical list of their mottos, with correct translations; a list of extinct baronets, and of those who have been advanced to the peerage; a list of persons who have received the honour of knighthood, and of British subjects possessing foreign orders of knighthood*, 2 vols. (London: F. C. & J. Rivington, 1808).
21. Alistair M. Duckworth, *The Improvement of the Estate: A Study of Jane Austen's Novels* (Baltimore: Johns Hopkins University Press, 1994); David Monaghan, '*Mansfield Park* and Evangelicalism: A Reassessment', in Ian Littlewood (ed.), *Jane Austen: Critical Assessments*, 4 vols. (Mountfield: Helm Information, 1998), iv. 167–79.

22. Northrop Frye, *Anatomy of Criticism: Four Essays* (Princeton: Princeton University Press, 1971), 186–203.
23. Susan Morgan, 'Why There is no Sex in Jane Austen's Fiction', *Studies in the Novel*, 19 (1987), 346–55.
24. Lawrence Stone, *Family, Sex and Marriage: The Family and Marriage in England, 1500–1800* (Harmondsworth: Penguin, 1985).
25. Quoted in E. J. Clery and Robert Miles (eds.), *Gothic Documents: A Sourcebook, 1700–1820* (Manchester: Manchester University Press, 2000), 89.
26. Quoted in ibid.
27. See Kate Ferguson Ellis, *The Contested Castle: Gothic Novels and the Subversion of Domestic Ideology* (Urbana, Ill.: University of Illinois Press, 1989), and Mary Poovey, *The Proper Lady and the Woman Writer: Ideology as Style in the Works of Mary Wollstonecraft, Mary Shelley, and Jane Austen* (Chicago: University of Chicago Press, 1984).

CONCLUSION

1. I paraphrase Deirdre Lynch, *The Economy of Character: Novels, Market Culture, and the Business of Inner Meaning* (Chicago: University of Chicago Press, 1998), 212.
2. Clifford Siskin, *The Work of Writing: Literature and Social Change in Britain, 1700–1830* (Baltimore: Johns Hopkins University Press, 1999), 1–26.
3. Benedict Anderson, *Imagined Communities* (London: Verso, 1983).
4. See Robert Miles, *Gothic Writing 1750–1820: A Genealogy*, 2nd edn. (Manchester: Manchester University Press, 2002), 48–53.
5. Katie Trumpener, *Bardic Nationalism: The Romantic Novel and the British Empire* (Princeton: Princeton University Press, 1997).
6. For further discussion of these issues, see Nick Groom, 'Forgery or Plagiarism? Unravelling Chatterton's Rowley', *Angelaki*, 1/2 (1993–4), 41–54; Ian Haywood, *The Making of History: A Study of the Literary Forgeries of James Macpherson and Thomas Chatterton in Relation to Eighteenth-Century Ideas of History and Fiction* (Rutherford, N J: Associated University Presses, 1986); and W. T. Scott, 'The Literary Fraud: An Intractable Problem for Law and Semiotics', in Roberta Kevelson (ed.), *Conscience, Consensus, and Crossroads in Law* (New York: Peter Lang, 1995), 291–313.
7. Paul Baines, *The House of Forgery in Eighteenth-Century Britain* (Aldershot: Ashgate, 1999).
8. Pierre Bourdieu, *Distinction: A Social Critique of the Judgement of Taste*, trans. Richard Nice (London: Routledge, 1984).

9. Jürgen Habermas, *The Structural Transformation of the Public Sphere: An Inquiry into a Category of Bourgeois Society*, trans. Thomas Burger with the assistance of Frederick Lawrence (Cambridge, Mass.; MIT Press, 1991).

10. Michel Foucault, 'What is an Author?', in Vincent B. Leitch (gen. ed.), *The Norton Anthology of Theory and Criticism* (New York: W. W. Norton & Co., 2001), 1622–6.

11. Richard B Sher, 'Printed by Strahan and Cadell: The Advertising Catalogues of Late Eighteenth-Century Britain's Leading Publishers', paper delivered at Print Culture in the Age of the Circulating Library, 1750–1850, Sheffield Hallam University, July 2001.

12. Lynch, *The Economy of Character*, 209–10.

13. Ibid. 221.

14. For a discussion of Susan Price's representation as an instance of Austen's ideological mystification of property, see Brean S. Hammond, 'The Political Unconscious in *Mansfield Park*', in Nigel Wood (ed.), *Mansfield Park* (Buckingham: Open University Press, 1993), 82.

15. Marilyn Butler, *Jane Austen and the War of Ideas* (1974; repr. Oxford: Clarendon Press, 1987); Jerome McGann, *Romantic Ideology: A Critical Investigation* (Chicago: University of Chicago Press, 1983), 31. McGann has revised his view in *The Poetics of Sensibility: A Revolution in Literary Style* (Oxford: Clarendon Press, 1996).

16. Quoted in Brian Southam (ed.), *Jane Austen: The Critical Heritage*, 2 vols. (London: Routledge & Kegan Paul, 1968), i, 58–69, 87–105.

17. Siskin, *The Work of Writing*, 202.

18. Brian Southam (ed.), *Jane Austen: The Critical Heritage, 1870–1940*, 2 vols. (London: Routledge & Kegan Paul, 1987), ii, 1–12.

19. See above, Ch. 4 n. 4.

20. Slavoj Zizek, 'Enjoy your Nation as Yourself!', in Zizek, *Tarrying with the Negative* (Durham, NC: Duke University Press, 1993), 202.

21. I discuss these problems at length in Robert Miles, 'Abjection, Nationalism and the Gothic', in Fred Botting (ed.), *Essays and Studies 2001: The Gothic* (Cambridge: D. S. Brewer, 2001), 47–70.

22. Lionel Trilling, 'Why we Read Jane Austen', in Trilling, *The Last Decade: Essays and Reviews, 1965–75*, ed. Diana Trilling (Oxford: Oxford University Press, 1982), 204–25.

23. Southam (ed.), *Jane Austen: The Critical Heritage*, ii. 12.

24. Q. D. Leavis, quoted in Roger Gard, *Jane Austen's Novels: The Art of Clarity* (Cambridge, Mass.: Harvard University Press, 1994), 14.

25. See above, Introduction n. 3.

26. For instance, see Marilyn Butler, Introduction, in *Northanger Abbey* (Harmondsworth: Penguin, 1995), p. xviii.
27. Ibid. 231 n. 89.
28. Siskin, *The Work of Writing*, 202.
29. Southam (ed.), *Jane Austen: The Critical Heritage*, ii. 1–12.
30. Quoted in ibid. 84.
31. Ibid. 58.
32. Ibid. 28–9.
33. Quoted in ibid. 61.
34. David Cannadine, 'The Palace of Westminster as the Palace of Varieties: Changing Images and Perceptions of Parliament from 1834', in Christine Riding and Jacqueline Riding (eds.), *The Houses of Parliament: History, Art, Architecture* (London: Merrell, 2000), 11–30.
35. Quoted in Southam (ed.), *Jane Austen: The Critical Heritage*, i. 129.

Select Bibliography

WORKS BY JANE AUSTEN

Sense and Sensibility (1811), ed. Ros Ballaster (Harmondsworth: Penguin, 1995).

Pride and Prejudice (1813), ed. Vivien Jones (Harmondsworth: Penguin, 1996).

Mansfield Park (1814), ed. Kathryn Sutherland (Harmondsworth: Penguin, 1996).

Emma (1816), ed. Fiona Stafford (Harmondsworth: Penguin, 1996).

Northanger Abbey (1818), ed. Marilyn Butler (Harmondsworth: Penguin, 1995).

Persuasion (1818), ed. Gillian Beer (Harmondsworth: Penguin, 1998).

Jane Austen's Letters to her Sister Cassandra and Others, ed. R. W. Chapman, 2nd edn. (Oxford: Oxford University Press, 1952).

BIOGRAPHY

Austen-Leigh, James Edward, *A Memoir of Jane Austen* (1870, rev. 1871), ed. R. W. Chapman (Oxford: Clarendon Press, 1926; repr. 1951). Jane Austen's nephew's hagiographical memoir was influential in creating the saintly image of 'Aunt Jane' that was widespread by the close of the nineteenth century.

Halperin, John, *The Life of Jane Austen* (Baltimore: Johns Hopkins University Press, 1996). A revisionist biography that aims to bring out Jane Austen's pricklier characteristics.

Honan, Park, *Jane Austen: Her Life* (London: Weidenfeld & Nicolson, 1987). The standard life of Jane Austen.

Nokes, David, *Jane Austen: A Life* (London: Fourth Estate, 1997). Follows Halperin, but probes the scandals of the Austen family in greater depth than Halperin does. Nokes closely examines the

Austen family's relationship to Warren Hastings, the disgraced Governor of British India; the trial of Jane Austen's aunt, Mrs Leigh-Perrot, for theft; and her brother, Henry's, bankruptcy.

Shields, Carol. *Jane Austen* (London: Weidenfeld & Nicolson, 2001). Carol Shields's concise biography offers a novelist's-eye view of the interrelationship between Austen's biography and her fiction.

CRITICISM

Anon., review of *Emma*, *Champion*, 31 Mar. 1816, 102–3; repr. *Nineteenth-Century Fiction*, 26/4 (Mar. 1972), 469–74.

Armstrong, Isobel, *Mansfield Park*, Penguin Critical Studies (Harmondsworth: Penguin, 1988). In this detailed study Isobel Armstrong challenges prevailing views on the political conservatism of *Mansfield Park*. Armstrong's study is particularly recommended for its close reading of how *Lover's Vows* works within the novel to open up its interpretative possibilities.

——'Introduction', in *Pride and Prejudice* (Oxford: Oxford University Press, 1998), pp. vii–xxvi.

Ballaster, Ros, Introduction, in *Sense and Sensibility* (Harmondsworth: Penguin, 1995).

Butler, Marilyn, *Jane Austen and the War of Ideas* (1974; repr. Oxford: Clarendon Press, 1987). A landmark study situating Austen's politics and fictional concerns within the context of the ideological debates raging in the aftermath of the French Revolution.

——Introduction, in *Northanger Abbey* (Harmondsworth: Penguin, 1995).

Castle, Terry, 'Sister, Sister', review of *Jane Austen's Letters*, ed. Deirdre Le Faye, *London Review of Books*, 3 Aug. 1995.

Copeland, Edward, 'Money', in Edward Copeland and Juliet McMaster (eds.), *The Cambridge Companion to Jane Austen* (Cambridge: Cambridge University Press, 1997), 131–48.

Duckworth, Alistair M., *The Improvement of the Estate: A Study of Jane Austen's Novels* (Baltimore: Johns Hopkins University Press, 1994). The standard work on the meaning of landscape in Austen's fiction.

Evans, Mary, *Jane Austen and the State* (London: Tavistock Publications, 1987). An important essay on the sociological meaning of Austen's novels.

Gard, Roger, *Jane Austen's Novels: The Art of Clarity* (Cambridge, Mass.: Harvard University Press, 1994). Gard's book is a combative defence of Austen's artistic supremacy in the field of the novel.

Hammond, Brean S., 'The Political Unconscious in *Mansfield Park*', in Nigel Wood (ed.), *Mansfield Park* (Buckingham: Open University Press, 1993), 56–87.

Handler, Richard, and Segal, Daniel, *Jane Austen and the Fiction of Culture: An Essay on the Narration of Social Realities*, 2nd edn. (Lanham, Md.: Rowman & Littlefield, 1999). An interdisciplinary work that brings the discipline of ethnography to bear upon Jane Austen's fiction.

Harding, D. W. *Regulated Hatred and Other Essays on Jane Austen*, ed. Monica Lawlor (London: Athlone Press, 1998). D. W. Harding was a member of F. R. Leavis's Scrutiny group, and a psychologist by training. This is a collection of his essays on Austen, including 'Regulated Hatred', which has had a powerful impact on Austen studies ever since its first appearance in 1940.

Johnson, Claudia L., *Jane Austen: Women, Politics and the Novel* (Chicago: University of Chicago Press, 1988). Johnson focuses on the sexual politics of novel writing in a revolutionary period: a highly influential feminist study of the author.

——'Austen Cults and Cultures', in Edward Copeland and Juliet McMaster (eds.), *The Cambridge Companion to Jane Austen* (Cambridge: Cambridge University Press, 1997), 211–26.

——and Stimson, Catharine R., *Equivocal Beings* (Chicago: University of Chicago Press, 1995).

Jones, Chris, ' "Nothing that did not Answer": Jane Austen and Romantic Interrogation', paper delivered at Sustaining Romanticism, Seventh International BARS Conference, Liverpool, July 2001.

Kelly, Gary, 'Religion and Politics', in Edward Copeland and Juliet McMaster (eds.), *The Cambridge Companion to Jane Austen* (Cambridge: Cambridge University Press, 1997), 149–69.

Kirkham, Margaret, *Jane Austen, Feminism and Fiction* (London: Athlone Press, 1997). First published in 1983, this is a pioneering work of feminist and Austen scholarship.

Leavis, Q. D., 'Jane Austen: Novelist of a Changing Society', in Leavis, *Collected Essays*, i. *The Englishness of the English Novel*, ed. G. Singh (Cambridge: Cambridge University Press, 1983), 26–60.

Lew, Joseph, ' "That Abominable Traffic": *Mansfield Park* and the Dynamics of Slavery', in Claudia L. Johnson (ed.), *Mansfield Park: A Norton Critical Edition* (New York: W. W. Norton & Co, 1997), 498–510. Originally published in Beth Fowkes Tobin (ed.), *History, Gender, & Eighteenth-Century Literature* (Athens, Ga.: University of Georgia Press, 1994), 271–300.

Looser, Devoney (ed.), *Jane Austen and Discourses of Feminism* (New York: St Martin's Press, 1995). A useful collection providing a representative selection of current feminist views on Austen.

165

Lynch, Deidre, *The Economy of Character: Novels, Market Culture, and the Business of Inner Meaning* (Chicago: University of Chicago Press, 1998). Lynch takes a print culture approach to novel writing of the Romantic period, including Jane Austen. One of the most influential recent studies on the context of Austen's writing.

——(ed.), *Janeites: Austen's Disciples and Devotees* (Princeton: Princeton University Press, 2000). This collection of essays is indispensable for anyone wishing to know more about the cultural meaning of the 'Janeite' phenomenon.

MacDonagh, Oliver, *Jane Austen: Real and Imagined Worlds* (New Haven: Yale University Press, 1991). Written by a historian, this is a full and illuminating study of how Austen's novels engage with Georgian society.

McMaster, Juliet, 'Class', in Edward Copeland and Juliet McMaster (eds.), *The Cambridge Companion to Jane Austen* (Cambridge: Cambridge University Press, 1997), 115–30.

——and Stovel, Bruce (eds.), *Jane Austen's Business: Her World and her Profession* (Basingstoke: Macmillan, 1996). Recommended for anyone interested in Austen's relationship to the developing role of the professional woman writer.

Mandal, Anthony, 'Jane Austen and the Production of Fiction, 1785–1818', unpublished Ph.D. thesis (University of Wales, 2001).

Miller, D. A. 'Austen's Attitude', *Yale Journal of Criticism: Interpretation in the Humanities*, 8 (1995), 1–5.

Monaghan, David, '*Mansfield Park* and Evangelicalism: A Reassessment', in Ian Littlewood (ed.), *Jane Austen: Critical Assessments*, 4 vols. (Mountfield: Helm Information, 1998), iv. 67–79.

Monaghan, Peter, 'Sex and Sensibility, Scholars Redefine Jane Austen', *Chronicle of Higher Education*, 17 Aug. 2001.

Morgan, Susan, *In the Meantime: Character and Perception in Jane Austen's Fiction* (Chicago: University of Chicago Press, 1980). Morgan's book provides numerous close readings of the meaning of social interactions as represented in Austen's novels.

——'Why There is no Sex in Jane Austen's Fiction', *Studies in the Novel*, 19 (1987), 346–55.

Murdrick, Marvin, *Jane Austen: Irony as Defense and Discovery* (Berkeley and Los Angeles: University of California Press, 1952). Murdrick extends the views of D. W. Harding by showing how Austen employed irony as a defence against her society.

Poovey, Mary, *The Proper Lady and the Woman Writer: Ideology as Style in the Works of Mary Wollstonecraft, Mary Shelley, and Jane Austen* (Chicago: University of Chicago Press, 1984). A landmark in feminist criticism, this study is still a standard work on what it meant for a woman to profess writing in the Romantic era.

Roberts, Warren, *Jane Austen and the French Revolution* (London: Athlone Press, 1995). Originally published in 1979, Warren's was one of the first studies to make the case that Austen took a sustained interest in the French Revolution and its consequences.

Sales, Roger, *Jane Austen and Representations of Regency England* (London: Routledge, 1994). Sales demonstrates how Austen's mature works engage with the Regency crisis that dominated political discussion of the day.

Southam, Brian (ed.), *Jane Austen: The Critical Heritage*, i (London: Routledge & Kegan Paul, 1968). Besides being an indispensable collection of reviews, Southam's two volumes contain substantial introductions that expertly put Austen's reception into perspective.

——(ed.), *Jane Austen: The Critical Heritage, 1870–1940*, ii (London: Routledge & Kegan Paul, 1987).

——'The Silence of the Bertrams', in Claudia L. Johnson (ed.), *Mansfield Park: A Norton Critical Edition* (New York: W. W. Norton & Co, 1997), 493–8. Originally published in the *Times Literary Supplement*, 17 Feb. 1995.

Trilling, Lionel, 'Why we Read Jane Austen', in Trilling, *The Last Decade: Essays and Reviews, 1965–75*, ed. Diana Trilling (Oxford: Oxford University Press, 1982), 204–25.

——'*Mansfield Park*', in Claudia L. Johnson (ed.), *Mansfield Park: A Norton Critical Edition* (New York: W. W. Norton & Co, 1997), 423–33; originally published in *The Opposing Self: Nine Essays in Criticism* (New York: Viking, 1955), 208–30.

BACKGROUND READING

Allott, Miriam, *Novelists on the Novel* (London: Routledge & Kegan Paul, 1959).

Anderson, Benedict, *Imagined Communities* (London: Verso, 1983).

Aristotle, 'On the Art of Poetry', in *Aristotle/Horace/Longinus: Classical Literary Criticism*, trans. T. S. Dorsch (Harmondsworth: Penguin, 1965).

Armstrong, Nancy, *Desire and Domestic Fiction: A Political History of the Novel* (Oxford: Oxford University Press, 1987).

Baines, Paul, *The House of Forgery in Eighteenth-Century Britain* (Aldershot: Ashgate, 1999).

Barrell, John, *Imagining the King's Death: Figurative Treason, Fantasies of Regicide, 1793–1796* (Oxford: Oxford University Press, 2000).

Bate, Jonathan, 'Faking It: Shakespeare and the 1790s', *Essays and Studies*, 46 (1993), 63–80.

Bayley, John, *The Characters of Love: A Study of the Literature of Personality* (London: Constable, 1960).

Bergson, Henri, *Laughter: An Essay on the Meaning of the Comic*, trans. Cloudesley Brereton (London: Macmillan, 1921).

Bewley, Marius, *The Eccentric Design: Form in the Classic American Novel* (New York: Columbia University Press, 1959).

Bloom, Harold, *Shakespeare: The Invention of the Human* (London: Fourth Estate, 1999).

Bourdieu, Pierre, *Distinction: A Social Critique of the Judgement of Taste*, trans. Richard Nice (London: Routledge, 1984).

Butler, Marilyn (ed.), *Burke, Paine, Godwin and the Revolution Controversy* (Cambridge: Cambridge University Press, 1984).

Cain, P. J., and Hopkins, A. G., *British Imperialism: Innovation and Expansion, 1688–1914* (London: Longman, 1993).

Cannadine, David, 'The Palace of Westminster as the Palace of Varieties: Changing Images and Perceptions of Parliament from 1834', in Christine Riding and Jacqueline Riding (eds.), *The Houses of Parliament: History, Art, Architecture* (London: Merrell, 2000), 11–30

Carter, Ronald (ed.), *Language and Literature: An Introductory Reader in Stylistics* (London: Routledge, 1991).

Clery, E. J., and Miles, Robert (eds.), *Gothic Documents: A Sourcebook, 1700–1820* (Manchester: Manchester University Press, 2000).

Colley, Linda, *Britons: Forging the Nation 1707–1837* (New Haven: Yale University Press, 1992).

Copeland, Edward, *Women Writing about Money: Women's Fiction in England, 1790–1820* (Cambridge: Cambridge University Press, 1995).

Ellis, Kate Ferguson, *The Contested Castle: Gothic Novels and the Subversion of Domestic Ideology* (Urbana, Ill.: University of Illinois Press, 1989).

Empson, William, *Some Versions of Pastoral* (London: Chatto & Windus, 1950).

——'Hamlet when New', *Sewanee Review*, 61 (1953), 15–42, 185–205.

Forster, E. M., *Aspects of the Novel* (London: E. Arnold, 1949).

Foucault, Michel, *The History of Sexuality*, i. *An Introduction*, trans. Robert Hurley (Harmondsworth: Penguin, 1979).

——'What is an Author?', in Vincent B. Leitch (gen. ed.), *The Norton Anthology of Theory and Criticism* (New York: W. W. Norton & Co., 2001), 1622–36.

Frye, Northrop, *Anatomy of Criticism: Four Essays* (Princeton: Princeton University Press, 1971).

Garside, Peter, 'The English Novel in the Romantic Era: Consolidation and Dispersal', in Peter Garside and Rainer Schöwerling (eds.), *The English Novel 1770–1829: A Bibliographical Survey of Prose Fiction Published in the British Isles*, ii. 1800–1829 (General Editors: Peter Garside, James Raven, and Rainer Schöwerling; Oxford: Oxford University Press, 2000), 15–103.

Gellner, Ernest, *Nations and Nationalism* (Oxford: Blackwell, 1983).

——*Nationalism* (London: Phoenix, 1998).

Groom, Nick, 'Forgery or Plagiarism? Unravelling Chatterton's Rowley', *Angelaki*, 1 / 2 (1993–4), 41–54.

Grossman, James, *James Fenimore Cooper* (London: Methuen & Co., 1950).

Habermas, Jürgen, *The Structural Transformation of the Public Sphere: An Inquiry into a Category of Bourgeois Society*, trans. Thomas Burger with the assistance of Frederick Lawrence (Cambridge, Mass.: MIT Press, 1991).

Hardy, Barbara, Introduction, in George Eliot, *Daniel Deronda* (Harmondsworth: Penguin, 1977).

Haywood, Ian, *The Making of History: A Study of the Literary Forgeries of James Macpherson and Thomas Chatterton in Relation to Eighteenth-Century Ideas of History and Fiction* (Rutherford, NJ: Associated University Presses, 1986).

——*Faking It: Art and the Politics of Forgery* (Brighton: Harvester Press, 1987).

Hobsbawm, E. J., *Nations and Nationalism since 1780: Programme, Myth and Reality* (Cambridge: Cambridge University Press, 1990).

Jones, Chris, *Radical Sensibility* (London: Routledge, 1993).

Kaul, A. N., *The American Vision: Actual and Ideal Society in Nineteenth-Century Fiction* (New Haven: Yale University Press, 1963).

Kelly, Gary, 'Religion and Politics', in Edward Copeland and Juliet McMaster (eds.), *The Cambridge Companion to Jane Austen* (Cambridge: Cambridge University Press, 1997), 149–69.

McCalman, Iain, *Radical Underworld: Prophets, Revolutionaries, and Pornographers in London* (Oxford: Clarendon Press, 1993).

McGann, Jerome, *Romantic Ideology: A Critical Investigation* (Chicago: University of Chicago Press, 1983).

——*The Poetics of Sensibility: A Revolution in Literary Style* (Oxford: Clarendon Press, 1996).

Marinelli, Peter, *The Pastoral* (London: Methuen, 1971).

Maturin, Charles Robert, *Women; or, Pour et contre* (Edinburgh: Archibald Constable, 1818).

Miles, Robert, 'Abjection, Nationalism and the Gothic', in Fred Botting (ed.), *Essays and Studies 2001: The Gothic* (Cambridge: D. S. Brewer, 2001), 47–70.

—— *Gothic Writing 1750–1820: A Genealogy*, 2nd edn. (Manchester: Manchester University Press, 2002).

Pascal, R., *The Dual Voice: Free Indirect Speech and its Functioning in the Nineteenth-Century European Novel* (Manchester: Manchester University Press, 1977).

Poirier, Richard, *A World Elsewhere: The Place of Style in American Literature* (Oxford: Oxford University Press, 1966).

Raven, James, 'The Novel Comes of Age', in James Raven and Antonia Fraser (eds.), *The English Novel 1770–1829: A Bibliographical Survey of Prose Fiction Published in the British Isles*, i. *1770–1779* (General Editors: Peter Garside, James Raven, and Rainer Schöwerling; Oxford: Oxford University Press, 2000), 15–121.

Rorty, Richard, 'Comments on Castoriadis's "The End of Philosophy"', *Salmagundi*, 82–3 (1989), 24–30.

Said, Edward, *Culture and Imperialism* (London: Chatto & Windus, 1993).

Schoenbaum, Samuel, *Shakespeare's Lives* (Oxford: Oxford University Press, 1970).

Scott, W. T., 'The Literary Fraud: An Intractable Problem for Law and Semiotics', in Roberta Kevelson (ed.), *In Conscience, Consensus, and Crossroads in Law* (New York: Peter Lang, 1995), 291–313.

Scott, Sir Walter, *The Journal of Sir Walter Scott*, ed. David Douglas, 2 vols. (Edinburgh, 1890).

Sekora, John, *Luxury: The Concept in Western Thought, Eden to Smollet* (Baltimore: Johns Hopkins University Press, 1977).

Sher, Richard B., 'Printed by Strahan and Cadell: The Advertising Catalogues of Late Eighteenth-Century Britain's Leading Publishers', paper delivered at Print Culture in the Age of the Circulating Library, 1750–1850, Sheffield Hallam University, July 2001.

Siskin, Clifford, 'A Formal Development: Austen, the Novel, and Romanticism', *Centennial Review*, 29 (1985), 1–28.

——*The Work of Writing: Literature and Social Change in Britain, 1700–1830* (Baltimore: Johns Hopkins University Press, 1999).

Stone, Lawrence, *Family, Sex and Marriage: The Family and Marriage in England, 1500–1800* (Harmondsworth: Penguin, 1985).

Todd, Janet, *Sensibility: An Introduction* (London: Methuen, 1986).

Trilling, Lionel, 'Manners, Morals, and the Novel', in Trilling, *The Liberal Imagination: Essays on Literature and Society* (London: Secker & Warburg, 1951), 205–22.

——'Art and Fortune', in Trilling, *The Liberal Imagination: Essays on Literature and Society* (London: Secker & Warburg, 1951), 255–80.

Trumpener, Katie, *Bardic Nationalism: The Romantic Novel and the British Empire* (Princeton: Princeton University Press, 1997).

Wales, Katie, *A Dictionary of Stylistics*, 2nd edn. (Harlow: Pearson Education, 2001).

Wollstonecraft, Mary, *The Vindications: 'The Rights of Men' and 'The Rights of Woman'*, ed. D. L. Macdonald and Kathleen Scherf (Peterborough, Ontario: Broadview Press, 1997).

Zizek, Slavoj, *Tarrying with the Negative* (Durham, NC: Duke University Press, 1993).

Index